DON'T MAKE HISTORY
CHANGE THE FUTURE

The call to live life 1-2-3

Centre for
Faith and Spirituality
Loughborough University

Join the movement now and begin your journey...
Sign up at www.livelife123.org
Follow on Twitter
@livelife123org and use #ilivelife123
to be part of the conversation on Twitter

LIKE the Facebook page
www.facebook.com/livelife123org

Matt Summerfield
msummerfield@urbansaints.org

I love the vision behind 1-2-3 - if we read this book and do what it says, we will mature, our mates will grow and God's Kingdom will begin to explode.

Andy Croft, Soul Survivor

Invest 60 minutes and discover how God can use you to change the future! Packed with practical wisdom and biblical insight, Matt paints a vision big enough and simple enough for us all to jump into!

Andy Frost, Director, Share Jesus International

This book has vision, passion and practical steps in Christian discipleship and ought to be in the hands of every Christian!

Lyndon Bowring, Executive Chairman, CARE

Matt Summerfield has a vision, and now he has written a brilliantly engaging book about it. Through raw honesty, scriptural understanding and pacy story-telling, Matt will have you racing to catch up with his passionate dream for the generations emerging and still to come.

Martin Saunders, Editor, Youthwork and Childrenswork Magazines

The only way we are truly going to change our nation is if we see more disciples who make disciples who make disciples… I love this little book, and Matt's heart to see that wonderful change come.

Andy Hawthorne, The Message

This book is dynamite! One hour in the company of this book and the Holy Spirit will change your life, and change the lives of others. If together we live out the vision of this book, we will change a generation! I'm up for it, are you?

Mark Russell, Church Army

I love it when I read a book and know that the author lives and breathes all that they are writing about. Matt's passion for passing on the baton to the next generation speaks loudly, clearly and incredibly practically from every page - give an hour to reading it and be inspired and equipped to spend a lifetime living it!

Ruth Hassall, Author of Growing Young Leaders

This book will stop you in your tracks. It's a challenge to all of us to run our race well, and to teach the younger generations to do the same.

Steve Clifford, General Director of
Evangelical Alliance

I could not put this brilliant book down and am now ready to go! This short and powerful read will change you. Read it, live it and build a lasting legacy.

Gavin Calver, YFC

If you can't cope with being inspired to your very core, consumed by a compelling vision and given simple yet effective steps to change the future for generations to come, then be very careful as you read this book! It's a one-hour read that can have life-changing consequences.

Carl Belcher, Ground Level

Matt is a great communicator who has managed to articulate a clear challenge to all Christians who take the future seriously. This book is really practical and straight to the point in helping us realise that how we live our lives in the present can have a profound impact on the future. It will encourage you to work out your unique role in God's beautiful, unfolding Kingdom.

Carl Tinnion, YWAM

In this superb book, Matt is encouraging us all to make a difference and create a legacy that has Kingdom value. To affect lives, to invest in others, to create a work that is not of us, but of lasting Kingdom value. That is what Jesus did! I recommend that this book is not just read, but lived.

Ian Bunce, Baptist Union of Great Britain

Don't Make History, Change the Future is a must for those who want to build legacy. A mark of a great leader is that they grow other leaders; this is a wonderful read for those who aspire to invest in future generations.

Jill Garrett, Leadership coach

This is a heartfelt, honest and vulnerable call to action from a man who has a passion for the next generation and has invested his life to see young lives impacted by the message of Jesus. Read it, pass it on, take note, take action. I'm excited and have great hope for the future!

Carl Beech, Christian Vision for Men (CVM)

I have seen the future in a vision and it is full of young people coming out of different backgrounds joining forces to reach souls and change their world. Visions are powerful because they bring the colourful pictures from tomorrow into today, over-riding the negatives of yesterday. Matt's vision is very compelling. If we listen and respond as the united church, we may well see the fullness of the Kingdom come in one generation.

Dr Jonathan Oloyede, National Day of Prayer

I know and love Matt well, and I know him to be a passionate practitioner. Not content to merely talk the talk from public platforms, Matt seeks with openness, integrity and humility, to walk the walk. I encourage you:

read this book and walk it with him.

Pete Gilbert, DNA (www.dna-uk.org)

Jesus spent his time in community, calling and training disciples to pass on his life to others. It was these disciples that founded the church and changed the world. Matt has not only written a profoundly moving and honest book; he has shared a vision that has the potential to inspire generations of disciples to change the future. Its simplicity is its genius. Jesus calls his disciples to give their lives away to others, Live Life 123 is something worth giving your life away for!

Phil Ball, ALOVE UK,
The Salvation Army for a New Generation

I wholeheartedly endorse "Live Life 1-2-3" as an excellent, concise and pragmatic approach to Kingdom discipleship.

Ruben King, New Testament Church of God

Throughout history women and men have made a difference to the world by influencing others one person at a time. We see this in Bible characters like Esther, Moses, Mary, Paul and Lydia. We also see it in people who came after these great role models of faith in Amy Carmichael, Martin Luther King, Gladys Aylward, Mother Theresa and Nelson Mandela. I am excited to see how this book can bring forward the next generation of people who under God write the history of the future. The book is simple, easy to read and has the potential to empower people both young and old to make a difference where they are'.

Sharon Prior, Catalyst Training

URBAN SAINTS

Third edition 2014.
Second edition 2013.
First published 2012.

Cover design & book layout by Suzi Hull
ISBN 978-0-9559277-6-8

Urban Saints Support Centre:
Kestin House, 45 Crescent Road,
Luton, Beds. LU2 0AH

Telephone: 01582 589850
Fax: 01582 721702
Email: email@urbansaints.org
Website: www.urbansaints.org

Urban Saints is the operating name of The Crusaders' Union, a company limited by guarantee and registered in England & Wales, company number 07771037, charity number 1144923, and in Scotland, charity number SCO39313.

Printed and bound in India by Authentic Media, Secunderabad 500 067, India
E-mail: printing@ombooks.org

DON'T MAKE HISTORY CHANGE THE FUTURE

The call to live life 1-2-3

Join the movement now and begin your journey...

Sign up at www.livelife123.org

Follow on Twitter
@livelife123org and use #ilivelife123
to be part of the conversation on Twitter

LIKE the Facebook page
www.facebook.com/livelife123org

Matt Summerfield
msummerfield@urbansaints.org

livelife123.org

DEDICATION

This book is dedicated to my Mum and Dad,
who live to make others succeed.
You guys are awesome and I love ya!

Contents

It all comes from here.

Every idea… every dream, is birthed in a moment.

A moment when something so significant happens, you know life will never quite be the same again.

For me that moment came on a cold winter's evening in November 2000. You'll have to read chapter 3 to find out what happened. Suffice to say, ever since that night, my heart has been burning with a dream to see a generation of gutsy, courageous and uncompromising young people rise up and become God's torch-bearers and baton-carriers to those not yet born. Good News people in a broken world!

A book can be a great way to communicate ideas and plans, but in the end it's only words. My prayer is that these words don't just *inform* you about the need to invest more in the next generation, but *transform* your thinking about the children and young people that God has put in your family, church, school and community. The impact that you could have on their lives is extraordinary.

Before you say *"But, I'm not a youth worker or a young person"*, let me assure you that this book is still absolutely for you. I'll reiterate that: **THIS BOOK IS FOR EVERYBODY**. Of course my hope is that in reading it you might catch some of my passion for the rising generation of children and young people, but ultimately the challenge here is to consider the legacy of your life; to inspire you to invest time in growing other people – whether they're 8, 18, 38 or 68 years old.

As we'll discover, the world is changed through normal people – people like you – who run their race well, and help others to do the same.

So, thanks for reading this book. I've deliberately kept it short so that you can read it within an hour or so, and more importantly, respond to it in the ways that God inspires you to.

For the sake of the future – let's get cracking!

 For further thoughts from Matt watch a short video at:

www.livelife123.org/itallcomesfromhere

1: The Future Matters

I was around six years old when I became an Elvis Presley fan. That may be hard to believe, but the truth is that I thought the King of Rock 'n' Roll was awesome. Given the opportunity I would happily break out in blasts of "Are You Lonesome Tonight?" or "Teddy Bear" for anybody who would care to listen. My mum even made me an Elvis Presley costume for a fancy dress party once.

Apparently, when Elvis sadly passed away in 1977, there were a handful of people across the world who actually earned their living impersonating him – around 170 of them. Interestingly, by the year 2000 that number had risen to over 85,000 people. Imagine that. 85,000 people across the world who were paid to impersonate Elvis. I was 30 years old but confess to not being one of them.

But here's a scary thought. If those growth trends were to continue, by the year 2019 one in three people across the world would be Elvis impersonators. More than two billion Elves (not Elvi). Could you be one of them? Do you care? Probably not, and in the grand scheme of things I think you're probably right to relax.

But the future does matter, right?

Not in terms of whether we'll all be shaking our hips singing "It's now or never", but in terms of the world that our children are destined to inherit.

One of the most well-known and anthemic songs by the Christian band Delirious? is History Maker. I've been to plenty of lively youth gigs over the years where I've witnessed hundreds of young people declaring at the top of their voices...

"I'M GONNA BE A 'HISTORY MAKER' IN THIS LAND!"

But the truth is this: whether they intend to be history makers or not - they all will be!

In fact, **every single one of us will make history**. The big question that we really have to grapple with is this...

What kind of history are we going to make?

Or maybe even that is the wrong question. Why do I say that? Because your history is someone else's future! Let me say that again...

YOUR HISTORY IS SOMEONE ELSE'S FUTURE!

So maybe the real question is not, 'what history will I make?' but 'what kind of future will I create? What legacy will I leave? What possibilities and opportunities will I have opened up for those who follow me?'

A study some years ago interviewed a group of people all aged over 95. They were asked what they would do differently if they could live their lives over again. The results were pretty revealing. These wise men and women nearing the end of their lives wished that...

They had risked more

They had reflected more

They had done more things that would live on after they were dead

That last point is interesting. They wished that they had left a legacy.

They wished that they had **passed on** something worthwhile.

They wished that they had created a better future.

Why? Because deep down we all care about what

happens in the future; about the world we'll leave behind for the generations who follow up and those still to come.

Or at least, we should.

QUESTIONS FOR REFLECTION

1. How seriously do you consider the kind of world you'll leave behind?

2. What kind of legacy do you hope to leave?

3. What are some of the things you don't want to be regretting on your death bed?

 For further thoughts from Matt watch a short video at:

www.livelife123.org/thefuturematters

2: Your Decisions About the Future Matter

There's a shocking story, recorded in 2 Kings 20:12-19, about King Hezekiah. This man, who reigned from Jerusalem, was one of the rare Kings of Judah who actually loved God and sought to live for Him. He removed the idols, was obedient to God, and experienced significant levels of God's favour and success during his reign. But then, as so easily can happen, he got a little proud.

Five hundred miles to the east, the King of Babylon had heard about the incredible city of Jerusalem where Hezekiah was enthroned. Intrigued by rumours of Jerusalem's glorious palace and temple, the Babylonian King sent a team of ambassadors to personally investigate, under the guise of bringing good wishes and gifts to celebrate Hezekiah's recovery from a recent life-threatening illness. When the ambassadors eventually arrived in Jerusalem, King Hezekiah didn't hold back in showing them *everything*. He proudly gave them a tour of the temple, the palace, the armoury – every significant and impressive part of the city. The bottom line here: he was showing off. There's absolutely no sense that he was giving glory to God for any of it.

When the Ambassadors from Babylon had seen enough, they returned home. As they were leaving, the prophet Isaiah decided to pay Hezekiah a visit.

"Who are those guys heading out the door?" Isaiah enquired, his voice loaded with concern about what had just happened.

"They are men from the distant land of Babylon who travelled just to see me and my Kingdom. Do you realise how famous I've become?" Hezekiah replied (ok, so if you read the text he doesn't exactly say this but trust me, that's what's in his heart).

"So what did you show them?" Isaiah asked, already sensing that a word from God was about to burst out of his mouth.

"Everything!" Hezekiah announced proudly, "I showed them everything!"

And with that, the Spirit of God so stirred Isaiah that he could not hold the word from God any longer.

"And the Lord tells you today Hekeziah that the Babylonians will return. And when they return they will take *everything*. It will all be carried off to Babylon. And what is not carried off will be destroyed. And while this won't happen until you've passed away, this is the legacy you leave to your children. Your children will be kidnapped, tortured and taken captive to Babylon. This is the future you have created for those who follow you".

Wow. How would you react to a word like that? If God told you that after you died an invading nation would come to your community, steal everything of value, destroy everything else and more importantly, take all your children away and torture some of them. How would you react to a word like that?

Hezekiah's response is totally shocking.

"This message you have given me from the Lord is good."

Good? Hezekiah, are you serious? Why do you think this is good? The text in verse 19 gives us the answer. Hezekiah thinks to himself "At least there will be peace and security during my lifetime."

Can you believe this?

Hezekiah has just been told that in the coming years his community will be destroyed and his children snatched away. Yet all he can think about is himself. "At least I'll be ok," he thinks.

I'm sure you're as horrified as I am by Hezekiah's indifference to the future he has created. Yet it's still true today that many people just *don't* care about the legacy they're leaving behind. Our consumerist culture thrives on mantras like "live for today", and "buy-now, pay-later".

But the future matters!

Our *indifference* is not the only reason why we don't create a better future. **I choose to believe that most people care about the future, but a great future won't happen by chance.** We have to be intentional. We have to be committed. But the enemies of commitment - *indifference, lethargy, complacency, forgetfulness...* dare I say *laziness* – all too easily conspire against us. If we're not careful, we too could end up as a bunch of 95 years olds looking back at our lives and thinking: *"I wish I'd done more."*

Hezekiah has no sense of commitment to, or concern for, the future generations. It's as if he's thinking to himself: "This world is going to get worse... but it doesn't matter because I won't be here." That's not the attitude that God wants us to have. He wants us to be committed to building a better world for future generations. To giving them a great inheritance; to leaving a positive legacy. The consequences of not doing so can be immense.

In 1 Chronicles 17 David, Israel's most beloved King, decides that he needs to build a temple for God. David feels bad that he's living in a beautiful palace while God is still being worshipped in a tent. So David informs the prophet Nathan of his intention to build the world's greatest temple for the One True God. At first, Nathan thinks this is a fantastic idea and cheers David on; God has other ideas, and that night speaks to Nathan in a dream.

The following day, Nathan returns to David to give him the news:

> *"David, the Lord God says to you today: 'I chose you to be the King of Israel. I've always been with you and I still have great plans for the rest of your life. But – you're not the one to build this great temple. After you've passed away, your son and heir will do this.'"*

Now David has a choice! Will he be like Hezekiah

and not care what happens next for his son? After all, David *really* wants to build the temple. Some of us might have expected David to say something to his son Solomon along the lines of: "Son, I really wanted to build this temple but God says I can't and that you're going to do it. So I'm going to leave you to it. Best of luck."

But David isn't like Hezekiah. Five chapters later we read of David's response to God's plans in 1 Chronicles 22:5:

> *"David said, 'My son Solomon is young and inexperienced, and the house to be built for the LORD should be of great magnificence and fame and splendor in the sight of all the nations. Therefore I will make preparations for it.' So David made extensive preparations before his death."*

Did you catch that? *"David made extensive preparations before his death"*. David was committed to doing everything he possibly could to set his son up to succeed. He wanted to leave the best legacy - the brightest future - for his son. This cost him a lot: time, money, talent, energy, passion, probably more than a few tears... the list goes on. Check that word 'extensive' again; it literally means abundant, numerous and multitudinous!

Hezekiah gave NOTHING.
David gave EVERYTHING.

Hezekiah lived for TODAY.
David prepared for TOMORROW.

Hezekiah was SELFISH.
David was SELFLESS.

You get the picture?

So the question is, who are you going to be? Hezekiah or David? Your decisions about the future matter.

QUESTIONS FOR REFLECTION

1. Think again about the things you don't want to have to list as regrets on your death bed. What can you do now to avoid those things becoming a reality?

2. How could you practically be less of a Hezekiah, and more of a David?

For further thoughts from Matt watch
a short video at:

www.livelife123.org/yourdecisionsmatter

3: God's Future Dream

It was late one evening in November 2000 and I was in the office alone. The Urban Saints movement (formerly known as Crusaders) had just spent several months developing a new five-year strategy, and as we neared the completion of this task I found myself asking God how the strategy for our organisation would fit into His bigger Kingdom plan to change a nation. As I prayed, I was reminded of this arresting scripture from Judges 2:10:

> *"After that whole generation had been gathered to their fathers, another generation grew up, who knew neither the LORD nor what he had done for Israel."*

How could this have happened? How could a generation of children and young people grow up in the footsteps of a leader such as Joshua without any knowledge of God and His mighty works? Moses seemed to have done so well to pass the baton to Joshua, and yet it seems that Joshua had dropped that baton and failed to create an equally great future for the generations that followed him. This scripture had always bothered me, but on this particular evening it had a clear prophetic ring to it.

As I reflected on the words of the passage it was not hard to see how it connected with the stark reality that over 90% of the children and young people in the UK and Ireland today have no regular meaningful contact with the church. A generation who neither know God or His goodness will reject Him out of ignorance rather than rebellion. To them, Jesus isn't the Saviour of the world. He's just a swear word.

Here's a bigger challenge though: unless something significant happens now, what will life be like in 20, 30 or 40 years time? What will happen to my children's children, and their children's children, unless the tide changes? How much of the future is my responsibility?

On that November night, I became so aware that God's vision is not only to see a generation of young people growing up with a real passion to follow Him, but also that they in turn would have a wholehearted commitment to pass His message on to future generations. He longs for a radical movement of young people, committed to taking the good news of Jesus Christ to everyone; a generation of gutsy, courageous and uncompromising young people who will become the torch bearers and baton carriers to those not yet born.

There's no clearer passage of scripture that describes God's vision:

> " ...We will tell the next generation about the glorious deeds of the LORD. We will tell of His power and the mighty miracles He did... so the next generation might know them - even the children not yet born... that they in turn might teach their children. So each generation can set its hope a new on God, remembering His glorious miracles and obeying His commands." (Psalm 78:4, 6, 7)

There it is! The vision of God – that each generation can set its hope anew on God, remembering His glorious miracles and obeying His commands.

It's the same message captured in Psalm 102 where, in v18 the writer dreams that "a people not yet born will praise the Lord." That's not making history, that's changing the future.

The Kingdom of God is moving forwards, not backwards. The message of the Gospel is that the life, death and resurrection of Jesus Christ deals with our broken, sinful **history** in order that we can embrace, and play our part in, God's great **future**.

God is in the business of changing the future – of our lives now and of our destinies – and He invites us to join in. Don't take my word for it - read the end of the Bible! Have you seen the amazing future that is careering towards us? Here's how Jesus' disciple John beautifully and poetically describes it in Revelation 21:

> *"Then I saw a new heaven and a new earth, for the old heaven and the old earth had disappeared. And the sea was also gone. And I saw the holy city, the new Jerusalem, coming down from God out of heaven like a bride beautifully dressed for her husband. I heard a loud shout from the throne, saying, 'Look, God's home is now among his people! He will live with them, and they will be his people. God himself will be with them. He will wipe every tear from their eyes, and there will be no more death or sorrow or crying or pain. All these things are gone forever.' And the one sitting on the throne said, 'Look, I am making everything new!'"*

This is our promised hope; this is our promised future. God's home will be among His people. It will be the end of sin, sickness, sadness and death. This is God's vision and nothing will stop it coming to pass. This is what we join in with today, so that we can work with God for a brighter tomorrow. Everything we do today which seeks to destroy the works of sin, sickness, sadness and death becomes a sign of God's coming future.

I love the way Tom Wright describes our partnership in God's future vision:

"*Every act of love, gratitude and kindness; every work of art or music inspired by the love of God and delight in the beauty of his creation; every minute spent teaching a severely handicapped child to read or to walk; every act of care and nurture, of comfort and support, for one's fellow human beings, and for that matter one's fellow non-human creatures; and of course every prayer, all Spirit-led teaching, every deed which spreads the gospel, builds up the church, embraces and embodies holiness rather than corruption, and makes the name of Jesus honoured in the world – all of this will find its way, through the resurrecting power of God, into the new creation which God will one day make. That is the logic of the mission of God. God's recreation of his wonderful world, which has begun with the resurrection of Jesus and continues mysteriously as God's people live in*

the risen Christ and in the power of the Spirit, means
that what we do in Christ and by the Spirit in the
present is not wasted."
- Tom Wright, from "Surprised by Hope" (2008)
  Used by permission from SPCK

The future matters.

Your decisions about the future matter.

Your decision to embrace, every day, God's vision for the future - matters.

QUESTIONS FOR REFLECTION

1. What do you think it will take for the rising generation of children and young people to set their hope on God?

2. How do you feel about the glimpses of God's Kingdom seen in Psalm 78, Revelation 21 and Tom Wright? What can you do to live these a little less as a dream, and a little more as reality?

For further thoughts from Matt watch a short video at:

www.livelife123.org/Godsdream

4: Redefining Big

It was a dark, early morning as I got up to get ready for work that day. In the interests of being a loving husband, I opted not to put our bedroom light on as I got changed, and sneaked out in the darkness as my newly wed wife slept on. It wasn't until later that morning that I realised that this had been a big mistake.

Imagine my horror as I sat at my computer screen and glanced down to discover that I had odd shoes on. To make matters worse, one of the shoes was brown while the other was black. They couldn't have been more different.

So now I was sitting in a busy open-plan office trying to hide my feet under the desk... and then my boss came along. We started to chat and because he was a good guy I decided to confess my wardrobe malfunction to him. This turned out to be my second mistake of the day. Ian laughed so loud that everybody in the office heard and looked up. For the rest of the day, as I walked up and down the corridor, waves of laughter followed close behind.

What an idiot!

Change the world? I can't even change my shoes!

Do you ever feel like that?

The world seems like a really big place. The future seems unending, with so many uncertain twists and turns. How could I possibly change the world? How could I possibly create a better future? It just seems too *big* a challenge.

But maybe – just maybe – we have the wrong understanding of *big*.

I wonder if you've ever had a conversation with someone where they have passionately declared "I want to do *big* things for God"? Perhaps you've said it yourself.

I know I have. I don't want to be a little candle burning in some small corner of the night. I want my life to be an Olympic torch for Jesus.

We all hear the stories of *big* churches, *big* events, *big* revivals, and of course, all of that is great. In my quest to be a future changer I long to see cities transformed, nations changed, churches full and events jam-packed with thousands. Yet is this really the *big* stuff in the eyes of our God?

Is this what we mean when we say 'I want to do *big* things for God"?

In Mark chapter 1, revival has come to Capernaum. Capernaum became like a base of operations for Jesus during His Galilean ministry. In Mark 1:21-34 we see details of Jesus' first visit to Capernaum where He caused quite a stir in just one day. In the morning He taught powerfully and with great authority in the synagogue, with people hanging on His every word. He then healed a man who was demonised, before going back to Peter's house for lunch, where He healed Peter's mother who was very sick with a fever. By early evening, news of His teaching authority and miraculous power had spread like wildfire across the whole area. Mark tells us that "the whole town" gathered at the door and that Jesus went on to heal various diseases and drive out demons.

As I said, revival has come to Capernaum!

In this moment Jesus secretly escapes, and goes to pray. He knows how important it is to remain connected to His Father. He knows He needs His Father's perspective on these things.

Some time later, Peter and the other disciples eventually find Jesus. Peter asks: "Where have you been? Everyone is looking for you." It's like Peter is saying to Jesus "This is *big*. This is massive. Revival has come to Capernaum. Let's set up camp. It's not going to get better than this – the whole town want to see you Jesus. This is *big*!"

I love Jesus' answer. Jesus says: "Nah! Let's go somewhere else!"

It kind of makes you wonder what's going on inside Jesus' head. How does Jesus define *big*? **Jesus appears to have a different definition of *big*.**

In the summer of 2008, I received a number of encouraging 'words' from people who informed me that I was about to be coming into a new season of increased influence for God. I was being told that I was approaching something *really big*.

It sounded exciting - but what did it mean? What would it look like?

It's easy to fall into the trap as a leader of a national movement to think that *big* is all about speaking on platforms, writing in magazines, and having influential meetings with 'important' people. Is that what Jesus ultimately defines as *big*? I don't think so, and I say this as someone who loves to preach, write, and network with others.

So I wondered, if God is really saying to me "Matt, your level of influence is about to significantly increase; you're coming in to something *big*" what was coming?

I started to get a sense of what God might be speaking about during a visit to New York and the former site of the World Trade Centre. The depth of sorrow and pain as I walked round the visitor centre, looking at photographs and quotes from September 11th 2001, was palpable. No-one spoke; people just slowly moved around the exhibition, soaking up the sadness.

As I walked out of the visitor centre I felt low, overwhelmed by this evil act. What hope is there for the world - for humanity, I wondered - when such acts of evil are performed? As I walked away I was reminded of the words of Paul in Romans 12:21:

> *"Do not be overcome by evil, but overcome evil with good."*

It's the acts of goodness and love that we do for people that overcome and overwhelm the works of evil in the world. Every act of kindness counts.

The next morning I found myself sitting alone in the departure lounge at Newark Airport when a lady sat down at the other end of the row. As I worked furiously on my laptop writing reports and responding to emails, I suddenly became aware that this lady was crying. Really crying.

And then it came.

The nudge of the Spirit.

I felt like God was telling me to stop what I was doing, and go and comfort this woman. I foolishly tried to reason with God and get myself off the hook. "God, I can see she's upset... but can't you see I'm working? These reports and emails are about Christian stuff too!" I've learnt over the years that God is often like a persistent woodpecker relentlessly knocking on a tree, so in the end with a slight sigh, I closed my laptop, walked over to the lady and sat down.

"Are you ok?" I asked. If I'm honest, I was hoping she would just say "yes" so that I could return to my work.

"Actually, no," she replied. "I've just put my 15 year-old son on a plane and he's away from home for the first time for two weeks. I know it's stupid but I'm going to miss him and I worry about him."

For the next few moments we chatted together.

I found myself expressing genuine empathy and words of comfort to this stranger, coupled with the promise to pray that they would both be ok. As she headed off after our chat she stood and squeezed my shoulder. "Thank you for being so kind," she said warmly.

In truth I felt like a bit of a fraud. She had no idea how hard God had to work to arrest me from my work. However, in that moment, as I watched her walk away I was reminded again of those words from Paul:

> "Do not be overcome by evil, but overcome evil with good."

It was Mother Teresa who once said, "We cannot do great things on this Earth, only small things with great love".

Perhaps in the Kingdom of God, *big* is not about huge crowds or city wide revivals; maybe *big* is about making yourself individually available to God. To go where He wants you to go; to say what He wants you to say; to reach who He wants you to reach; to do what He wants you to do.

Maybe in the Kingdom, *big* is more about sharing your life with someone; bringing hope, help and encouragement. Many small acts of kindness today begin to create a better tomorrow.

In October 2008 I started volunteering again as a youth leader in my local church. We'd re-launched our outreach work as an Urban Saints group, and we were hugely encouraged to see so many young people come who knew nothing about Jesus and had no previous connection to church.

The words "you're coming into something *big*; your level of influence is about to increase massively" were still ringing in my ears... and then it hit me. It hit me as I packed away one Friday evening in early November after our Urban Saints Hitchin meeting that night.

Earlier that evening we'd been talking about the future, and we'd asked the young people to draw a picture which they believed summarised their future. We then invited the young people to share what they had drawn. One of our younger teens - I'll call her Sarah - declared to the rest of the group that she had drawn a picture of herself, age 30, living in a trailer park. As far as she was concerned her future was that she would just be 'trailer trash'.

After the meeting I went up to Sarah and said to her, "I never want to hear you speak like that about yourself. You are not trailer trash. You will never be trailer trash. You are very special. We think you're awesome. God thinks you're awesome. I never want to hear you speak like that about yourself again. We believe in you." As I said these words, she pulled the hat that she was wearing down over her eyes, but not quickly enough to hide the tears that started to slide down either cheek.

So half an hour later I was packing away, when suddenly it hit me like a punch in the face. Of course! It's not about platforms, or books, or meetings – it's about these young people. It's about this group of young people from my home town who God has connected me to; who I get to 'do life' with.

Big in the Kingdom of God is about seeing an individual's life transformed by the Good News of Jesus.

Sure, I can influence people by preaching and writing and attending meetings, but those are rare moments of influence; they do not last, and much of them will be forgotten. Every week though, I hope for years to come, I get to share my life – invest my life – in a group of young people who God has entrusted into our care. I get to partner with God for years to come to see their lives change. There's nothing greater; there's nothing bigger; there's nothing more influential than seeing one life transformed with the good news of Jesus through the commitment of a life-long relationship.

Jesus lived a life that shone like the sun, attracting thousands who would flock to hear Him or be healed by Him, yet He poured His life into just a handful of people. Why? Because this was the greatest thing He could do. This was the greatest influence He could bring.

Jesus was not driven by what we might think is *big*. For Him, *big* was investing in a handful of people who He believed could change the world.

That's exactly what He invites **us** to do. What an awesome responsibility and privilege!

The disciples in Mark 1 said, "Jesus we have a great crowd; this is revival town, let's stick around!" Jesus said, "Let's go somewhere else. There are more people who need to hear, and more importantly than that, if we stay here you won't grow. You won't learn, you won't be changed, and you won't be challenged. I have come to invest in you – not the crowd – so follow me and let's continue on in this adventure."

How do you change the world?

How do you change the future?

One life at a time.

Still not convinced? Let me share my all-time favourite story as I bring this chapter to a close.

It was 1858, and a Boston Sunday School teacher named Kimball began visiting one of his students at a local shoe shop where the lad worked as a clerk. Through his faithful commitment Kimball eventually had the privilege of leading the young boy to Christ.

The young man's name was DL Moody.

DL Moody grew up to become a powerful evangelist and some 21 years later found himself in London leading a great spiritual awakening. A local London minister by the name of FB Meyer went along to hear Moody preach and was profoundly moved and affected by God's call on the man. Years later, Meyer found himself in the USA, where a young student by the name of J. Wilbur Chapman became a Christian at one of Meyer's meetings.

Chapman became heavily involved in the YMCA, and during his time there, met and discipled a former baseball player called Billy Sunday. Billy Sunday became another great evangelist and during one of his crusades in a small town called Charlotte led many to Christ.

The following year the people who had found Christ at the Billy Sunday crusades organised another crusade, inviting another eminent evangelist called Mordecai Hamm to speak. Hamm left the town three weeks later feeling discouraged due to the fact that only a handful of people had come to faith in Christ.

But one of those new Christians was a teenage boy called Billy Graham... who went on to lead literally millions of people to Jesus, all over the world.

The point of the story is ultimately not about Billy Graham. It's about an unknown school teacher called Kimball, who nearly one hundred years earlier committed to invest in DL Moody. Just one boy. One life.

Because Kimball did that he changed the future, for millions of people.

How do you change the world? How do you change the future?

One life at a time. We can all do that, can't we?

QUESTIONS FOR REFLECTION

1. Be honest with yourself: how do you define big when it comes to serving God?

2. How do you need to adjust your definition of what really matters?

3. Who are some of the people you are immediately feeling prompted to invest your life in?

 For further thoughts from Matt watch a short video at:

www.livelife123.org/redefiningbig

5: On Your Marks... Get Set... Go

I've never been very good at sports; particularly any that require great levels of speed and agility. My old PE teacher once told me that my turns in football reminded him of a large ferry boat swinging around in the middle of the sea. I don't think this was intended as a compliment.

I could run though. Not the 100m or 200m, but I had the endurance for the 1,500m.

Numerous times throughout the New Testament we're told that the Christian life is like a race. Paul writes in Acts 20:24:

> *"I consider my life worth nothing to me, if only I may finish the race and complete the task the Lord Jesus has given me"*

Again in 1 Corinthians 9:24, he says:

> *"Do you not know that in a race all the runners run, but only one gets the prize? Run in such a way as to get the prize."*

In Galatians 5:7 he asks:

> *"You were running a good race. Who cut in on you and kept you from obeying the truth?"*

And then whoever wrote Hebrews (and some people think it was also Paul) says in chapter 12 verse 1:

> *"...let us run with perseverance the race marked out for us."*

Life **is** a race then, but what kind of race? It's certainly not a 100m dash.

It's a marathon.

I've never run a marathon, although my Dad did a few years ago, putting me to shame. Afterwards he shared how there were moments in the marathon where he felt so strong, fit and energised that he thought he just couldn't lose. Then there were also moments of difficulty, pain, even agony, where he felt like he couldn't go on.

That sounds a lot like life, doesn't it? Full of highs and lows; mountain-top moments and valley experiences. Sunshine and rain; joys and sorrows.

Yet the race of life and faith is not just any marathon. It's a marathon relay (they do exist - I checked)! In 2 Timothy 2:2, the Apostle Paul, one of the most famous future changers, writes to his friend and mentee Timothy from a death row prison cell in Rome:

> *"You have heard me teach things that have been confirmed by many reliable witnesses. Now teach these truths to other trustworthy people who will be able to pass them on to others."*

Paul is saying, "Timothy, I've passed the baton of faith to you. Make sure you pass that baton on to others and then envision, equip and empower them to do the same."

It's a baton-passing, marathon relay. Just like in the story of Kimball, DL Moody and Billy Graham in the previous chapter.

Now remember, you get one chance to run your race of life and faith. This is not a rehearsal. You cannot go back and re-run it. Yesterday is history.

So with that picture of a marathon relay in mind I want to share four important principles for living a future changing life.

Run YOUR race.
Run your race WELL.
Pass the BATON on.
CHEER like crazy.

So the starting pistol has fired... let's get cracking.

QUESTIONS FOR REFLECTION:

1. As you reflect on the idea of a race as a metaphor for the Christian life, how is your race going? Are you running well, or flagging – desperate for water – even wondering whether to stop? Are you encouraging the other runners, or trying to trip them up? Are you racing ahead in the lead, jogging along in the middle, or bringing up the rear?

2. Whatever stage of the race you're at, however you're running – ask God again now for everything you need to continue running well.

 For further thoughts from Matt watch a short video at:

www.livelife123.org/onyourmarks

6: Run YOUR Race

When I was growing up as a teenager I longed to be able to dance like Michael Jackson, to have the body of Arnold Schwarzenegger, and the looks of John Taylor from Duran Duran (my then-girlfriend, now-wife fancied him). I took the 'body image' issue quite seriously and from the age of around 13 I was 'pumping iron' at least three times per week and drinking as much full fat milk as was humanly possible. At least, until one of the nastiest moments of my life occurred...

I've never been a very good 'morning' person and on this particular school morning I headed downstairs and sleepily got myself a glass of milk. We used to have these long blue glasses in our cupboard which could hold a full pint. As I sat at our breakfast table starting to gulp down this muscle-building liquid, I suddenly became aware that there was something else in my mouth other than just milk – and I don't mean my tongue.

I rolled what appeared to be a large ball of fluff to the tip of my tongue and then placed it on the breakfast table in front of me. When it landed, I quickly realised that this was not a ball of fluff at all, but actually a very large half-drowned, milk-covered spider, that had obviously fallen in to the glass; in my sleepiness I hadn't noticed. I can honestly tell you that I've not drunk milk since. (Apologies if this story has caused a slight gag reflex!)

It's good and right for us to look after our bodies, yet the sad fact is that I was like most teenagers – and dare I say a lot of adults too – who spend their lives crippled by comparison.

Wishing they were someone else.

I love the story in John 21, where Peter and Jesus are taking a walk on the beach after enjoying a fishy breakfast. Jesus is telling Peter about his future and the disciple John is walking a few yards behind them. As they walk together, Peter stops and looks back at John.

"What are your plans for John, Lord?" Peter asks.

I love Jesus' reply (paraphrased here). "Mind your own business. You concern yourself with my plan for your life and stop looking over your shoulder to see what others are up to."

That's good advice.

From time to time, I get asked to take assemblies in local Secondary schools. If it's my first ever visit (which is always possibly my last), I tend to give the same key talk every time. I do that because I believe it's one of the most important messages that young people need to hear. Perhaps you too need to hear it today, because here is a life-changing truth:

There will never be another YOU in the history of the human race.

The world needs you to stand up and take your place.

The sound of your life must be heard.

Grab hold of everything God created you to be.

God made you and He doesn't make mistakes.

Embrace the life you were born to live.

Don't waste another moment of your life trying to be someone else .

Be who you are – and start today!

What you do with your life matters... really matters!

For today - and for tomorrow.

I can't put it better than Paul when he writes in Ephesians 2:10:

> *"For we are God's masterpiece. He has created us anew in Christ Jesus, so we can do the good things he planned for us long ago."* (NLT)

If we're going to run our marathon relay well, becoming future changers, then we had better make sure we're running **our** race, not trying to run someone else's. As I've already said, comparison can cripple us!

Dare you believe that Ephesians 2:10 is true for you today? That you are God's masterpiece?

You are.

You may have been told by your parents that you were a mistake; that they didn't plan you. Your teachers may have said that you'll never amount to much.

God knows different. He knew you were coming. He has a destiny that has your name on it and no-one else in the history of planet earth can live out that destiny but you.

In fact, you were born a winner. You were conceived in your mother's womb because you literally won your first race, beating millions of fellow competitors who were trying to get there first.

This is the message that God gives to a teenage boy called Jeremiah, who later goes on to become one of Israel's greatest prophets. In Jeremiah 1:5 God tells the young man:

> "*I knew you before I formed you in your mother's womb. Before you were born I set you apart and appointed you as my prophet to the nations.*"

Likewise, King David writes in Psalm 139:14 that we are '*fearfully and wonderfully made.*'

God made you. He doesn't make mistakes. He doesn't make junk. You are unique, precious and beautiful. You were born for a purpose. You have a special mix of gifts and talents (of course you have weaknesses too; none of us can be great at everything).

So be thankful for who you are. Be thankful for the gifts God has given you. Be thankful that you are unique and precious to God. Be thankful that you can make your own unique mark in the world.

Author and professor Leo Buscaglia once said "The easiest thing to be in the world is you. The most difficult thing to be is what other people want you to be. Don't let them put you in that position."

The future needs you to rise up and take your place.

It starts right now - with you.

No-one else can make your mark on the world.

Run YOUR race, and stop comparing yourself with others.

QUESTIONS FOR REFLECTION

1. Be honest with yourself – how do you react to the Bible telling you that you are 'God's masterpiece'?

2. What can you do to see yourself more like God does?

3. What are some of the gifts and talents that God has given you?

 For further thoughts from Matt watch a short video at:

www.livelife123.org/runyourrace

Poem: We Trusted You

In Chapter 7 we're going to explore the importance of not just running OUR race but running it WELL. But before we get to that, I want to share a very challenging poem that was written by a teenager. It's a great reminder about why running our race **well** is so important. It's part of the legacy we leave. The future we create.

Beware, it may make for uncomfortable reading...

We Trusted You

We trusted you to live healthy lives before our conception; you abused yourselves with abnormal sex, drugs and nicotine

We trusted you for nourishment, but you fed us contamination

We trusted you to keep our bodies pure, but you made us addicts

We trusted you with our safety, but you passed laws to abort our lives

We trusted you with our future, but you gave us AIDS

We trusted you for love and affection, and you left us abandoned

We trusted you for a healthy diet and you cop out with junk food

We trusted you for our moral guidance and you set a pathetic example

We trusted you with our spiritual well being, and you never even mention Jesus

We trusted you with our education, and yet you let our schools fall apart

We trusted you to keep our eyes pure and yet you make films of explicit sex and violence

We trusted you to keep our ears pure, and yet you swear and blaspheme in front of us

We trusted you to keep our mouths pure and yet you feed us obscene literature and songs to recite

We trusted you with our young hearts and yet you

encourage us to grow old before our time

We trusted you with our mental welfare but you screwed up our minds with your double standards

We trusted you on building relationships and yet you locked us away inside video games

We trusted you to show us truth and you gave us virtual reality

We trusted you with family values and you gave us common law partners

We trusted you with our innocence but you abused our bodies

We trusted you with our adolescence; you encouraged us to have safe sex and contraception

We trusted you for what's right and what's wrong; you mock what's right and defend what's wrong

With our future - what future? We trusted you.

Challenging words. A little upsetting maybe. Perhaps you disagree with what's been written?

What future?

It's not too late to change it.

QUESTIONS FOR REFLECTION

1. How do the words of this poem make you feel?

2. Do they ring true? What lines of the poem challenged you or resonated with you the most?

3. What one thing could you try to do in reponse to the challenge that this poem has laid down?

7: Run Your Race WELL

If you stop any child, young person or adult in the street today and ask them for the first word that comes in to their head when you say "church" or "Christianity" I guarantee 95% will give the same answer. Any ideas what that might be?

"Boring!"

Closely followed by "irrelevant", I would imagine.

"Boring and irrelevant." That's what most people outside the church think today, which raises a huge question: how could that possibly have happened?

How has the radical, risk-embracing, world-changing, danger-accepting Jesus ended up looking so tame, safe and irrelevant?

Episcopal priest Robert Cappon put it this way:

> "What happened to the radical Christianity that turned the world upside down? What happened

to the category-smashing, life-threatening, anti-institutional gospel that spread through the first century like wild-fire? And was considered by those in power – 'dangerous'? What happened to the kind of Christians whose hearts were on fire, who had no fear, who spoke the truth no matter what the consequence; who made the world uncomfortable; who were willing to follow Jesus wherever He went? What happened to the kind of Christians who were filled with passion and gratitude and who, every day, were unable to get over the grace of God?"

If you were following Jesus' example, or that of the Apostle Paul, you knew that you were not embracing boredom but a life of risk, adventure, danger, excitement, joy and pain.

In his book, *The Barbarian Way,* Erwin McManus says "If our children are going to walk away from Christ, we need to raise them in such a way that they understand that to walk away from Jesus is to walk away from a life of faith, risk and adventure and to choose a life that is boring, mundane and ordinary."

If we're going to be future changers then we must not only run OUR race – but we must run it WELL.

It's time to think about the example that you are setting to the generation following you. What does it mean and what does it looks like - to be a follower of Jesus? Are you having a positive influence on the rising generation?

A few years ago I had the privilege of spending some time with a group of young people at a church in Dorset. They spent about half an hour or so asking me questions which ranged from 'If you were a fruit which fruit would you be?' to 'How did you become a Christian?' to 'Can you touch the ceiling with your hands?' I tried; I couldn't.

Then someone asked me: "What's the most radical thing you have ever done?"

Which was a great question. A tough question.

I could feel my brain creaking as it searched through the annals of my memory, trying desperately to find an inspiring, radical God-moment in my life.

In the end I told them a couple of stories of how I had stepped out in faith with God, where I had responded to something I felt He wanted me to do – to help someone else.

Even as I drove home later though, the question kept ringing in my ears: what's the most radical thing you have ever done? And then I remembered that I once heard someone say:

"You will only ever know that Jesus Christ is truly Lord – boss – of your life, if you want to go one way, and He wants you to go the other way – and you choose His way."

We're wired, aren't we, to look after number one? To serve ourselves; to be selfish and self-centred. We want to be Lord of our own lives.

Yet when we decide to follow Jesus, we put Him in the driving seat. At least... we're *supposed* to.

John tells us that during Jesus' time on earth, He said that He only did what He saw the Father doing. He only said what He heard the Father saying. He only went where He saw the Father going.

Then there's that ultimate moment – in the garden of Gethsemane – where the honesty of Jesus' humanity rages against the magnitude of God's mission. "If there's any other way Father," Jesus says. Then though, he utters those words of submission to God: "Not my will; your will."

That's the radical life – to be a person who says to God "Not my will, your will".

I'm going to do what I believe God wants me to do. I'm going to go where I believe God wants me to go. I'm going to be what God created me to be. I'm

going to speak out on what I believe God wants me to speak out. I'm going to live by God's agenda – and not my own.

Every time we make God choices, that is: every time we say 'yes' to God even though in our broken humanity we want to say 'no'... Every time – that's radical. That's our example.

Interestingly, the word 'Christian' appears only three times in the Bible, and yet the word 'disciple' features over 260 times throughout the New Testament. The original Greek word for disciple is *'mathetes'* which means 'learner' or 'student'. In fact, the best description would be 'apprentice.'

When Jesus calls men and women to be His disciples, He is inviting them to become His apprentices; His students. But He's not looking to impart skills and knowledge. Jesus may have been a carpenter, but His chief concern is not that you will score an A* in woodwork.

Jesus invites us to begin a journey where His way of life, becomes our way of life; a journey of transformation. A journey through which - with the help of the Holy Spirit - we would begin to think the way He thinks, do what He does, say what He says, go where He goes, and feel what He feels. A journey through which we would become **Christ-like,** becoming Jesus' future-shaping, agents of change in the world. That's why John wrote in 1 John 2:6 that:

> *"...those who say they live in God should live their lives as Jesus did."*

To run your race well means that you are committed to live like Jesus. Why is this so important? Because Jesus stands out as the central figure of human history. He is the centre-piece of time itself. Who He was, what He said, what He did, resulted in the future being changed! He is our example.

Paul was a devoted follower of Jesus, trying to live like Him in the world. Yet he dared to write to the church in Corinth:

> *"Follow my example, as I follow the example of Christ."* (1 Corinthians 11:1)

He issues a similar invitation to the church in Philippi:

> *"Join with others in following my example, brothers"* (Philippians 3:17)

And then again:

> "*Whatever you have learned or received or heard from me, or seen in me - put it into practice*" (Philippians 4:9)

Paul is clearly saying, "If you want to know what it looks like to be a follower of Jesus, then you won't go far wrong if you follow my example. I'm running my race well. Follow me, and I'll show you how to do the same."

Now before you starting worrying that Paul has a pride issue, chill out! Paul is very honest elsewhere about his faults, failings and continual struggles with sin. But the point is he's committed to be a learner; he is Jesus' apprentice. As he seeks to run his race well, he's committed to being a great example to others.

In his successes, he's committed to being an example.
In his struggles, he's committed to being an example.
In his suffering, he's committed to being an example.

Dare you be an example and inspiration to others, so that you too can say: "Follow me as I seek to follow Christ"? I find that extremely challenging, but I also want to commit to the responsibility of running my marathon relay well.

Let me underscore again that this is not about being perfect; none of us are. It's about being honest, authentic, vulnerable, humble, and responsible. It's about holding on to God whether life is good, bad or ugly. It's about being real about our struggles with faith and doubt.

I remember the day that my wife Jo went in to labour with our first son. I was actually doing a sponsored walk at the time, raising money for our youth group. My final mile of walking was abruptly interrupted when my father-in-law drove up declaring that I better get my wife to hospital quickly as she appeared to be going in to labour. Before I knew it, I was heading to the Maternity Unit with Jo, both of us feeling a mix of excitement and anxiety. Probably, more 'anxiety' if I'm honest!

When we arrived, they whisked Jo in to a room and put a heart monitor on the baby to check that all was well. It was then that it became clear that something wasn't quite right! Our baby's heartbeat was worryingly inconsistent. Sometimes it sounded normal and healthy, and then in other moments it would become slower and slower, our fear building as the gap between each beat grew larger – until it seemed to suddenly spring back in to life again.

"There's a chance the umbilical chord is wrapped around your baby's neck," the midwife told us, "We'll monitor what happens and decide what to do!"

I remember like it was just yesterday, sitting in that Maternity room, listening to every beat of our baby's heart. Praying "God, please don't let my baby die!"

Over twelve hours later, despite a very difficult birth, Andrew James Summerfield was born, and now he's nearly twenty-one years old.

It was slightly less than two years later when Jo became expectant with our second child. We were both thrilled and all was going well - until Jo woke me up in the middle of the night feeling that something was very wrong. The sight of severe bleeding didn't fill us with great confidence – or hope!

We drove to the hospital and soon found ourselves in a darkened room preparing for a scan. Again, I remember to this day the nurse performing the scan as I gripped my wife's hand – and then clenched my teeth to be as strong as I could for her, when the nurse told us "I'm really sorry, but you've lost your baby."

We drove home in silence and then as we stepped in to the house I remember us holding each other tightly in our front room. And yet there, in that moment – against all odds – we felt an incredible sense of God's peace, and the assurance that our loss was Heaven's gain. A deep sense of knowing that our child was with God.

I don't understand the reasons for everything that happens in our lives. Sometimes I can wrestle with doubt like anyone else. But this I do know! I know that God is always with us and He has what we really need – whether it's peace, hope, comfort, or love, to name but a few.

Running your race well - living like and following Jesus – does not mean you have a picture perfect life to role model to others. Far from it! Running your race well is about being committed to be the best possible example you can be; to keep learning, to keep growing, to be honest, to be real – whatever happens.

People like this are over-comers; they teach the generations to come to do the same. And that bodes well for the future.

QUESTIONS FOR REFLECTION

1. What does it mean; what does it look like, to be a follower of Jesus?

2. As you seek to lead others, how seriously do you take your own faith and example?

For further thoughts from Matt watch a short video at:

www.livelife123.org/runyourracewell

8: When the Ceiling Becomes the Floor

"We've never done it that way before!"

Don't you just hate that phrase? Doesn't it stifle creativity and opportunity? It's the kind of language that puts a lid, or a ceiling, on things.

It's not the language of future changers!

People who have committed to run **their** race and run it **well** understand that part of their responsibility is to set up the next generation for greater success.

They lift the lid.

The ceiling of their experience and achievement

becomes the floor for those who follow.

They're not satisfied, however, with creating a low ceiling. They're committed to setting the highest possible ceiling as their example, so that it will stretch and challenge the coming generation to go even further.

People said that it was impossible to run a mile in less than four minutes. Doctors suggested that the human heart would explode under the pressure. Yet on the 6th of May 1954, three thousand people watched Roger Bannister do what no-one thought was possible: he ran the mile in 3 minutes, 59.4 seconds.

That's not the end of the story though. Within 46 days, Bannister's record had been broken, and so followed many other athletes who ran the mile in less than 4 minutes, all because Roger had set a new standard. He lifted the lid; he broke through the perceived 'barriers'; he created new opportunities for those who followed after him.

People said that it was impossible to climb Mount Everest, the highest mountain in the world. Edmund Hillary disagreed, and so at 11:30 on the morning of May 29, 1953, Hillary and his fellow climber Tenzing Norgay reached the summit; 29,028 feet above sea level and the highest spot on earth. It was Hillary's third attempt at reaching the summit. Hillary set a new standard, and many others have followed in the years since.

If you had told people back in 1910 that one day athletes would high jump over eight feet, then they would've laughed in your face. At the time, athletes approached the high jump with a 'scissors style' and no-one managed to jump much higher than six feet. Between 1920 and 1950 a new technique was introduced – 'the western roll' – and athletes started jumping up to seven feet.

Then in the mid-50s to mid-60s the 'straddle' technique yielded results of up to seven and a half feet, until Dick Fosbury introduced his 'Fosbury Flop' in 1965 which now means that athletes break through the eight-foot barrier.

Step changes. Breakthroughs. New opportunities. Encouraging and inspiring the next generation to go even further. Living without limits. Remember King David; committed to setting up his son Solomon for even greater success.

That's the heart-beat of a future changer who - as they prepare to pass on the baton – hope and pray and work to see the next runner take things to a whole new level.

What does that mean for you today?

What does it look like for you to be a lid-lifter?

What does it look like for you to create a high ceiling which becomes the floor for others?

Where do you need to stretch yourself so that your example stretches others?

Don't settle for average. Give it your best shot. As AW Tozer once said:

"Refuse to be average. Let your heart soar as high as it will."

Remember that this is far more about who you are than what you do; character more than competence.

For example, if we all lived out these inspiring words from Romans 12:9-21 (from The Message version) it would bode well for future generations:

> *"Love from the centre of who you are; don't fake it. Run for dear life from evil; hold on for dear life to good. Be good friends who love deeply; practice playing second fiddle. Don't burn out; keep yourselves fuelled and aflame. Be alert servants of the Master, cheerfully expectant. Don't quit in hard times; pray all the harder. Help needy Christians;*

be inventive in hospitality. Bless your enemies; no cursing under your breath. Laugh with your happy friends when they're happy; share tears when they're down. Get along with each other; don't be stuck-up. Make friends with nobodies; don't be the great somebody. Don't hit back; discover beauty in everyone. If you've got it in you, get along with everybody. Don't insist on getting even; that's not for you to do. 'I'll do the judging,' says God. 'I'll take care of it.' Our Scriptures tell us that if you see your enemy hungry, go buy that person lunch, or if he's thirsty, get him a drink. Your generosity will surprise him with goodness. Don't let evil get the best of you; get the best of evil by doing good."

That's the way of Jesus.

So I pray: Lord, fill us with your Spirit **every day** so that we are empowered by you to create the highest possible ceiling in our lives, that will then become the floor to those who will receive the baton from us.

QUESTIONS FOR REFLECTION

1. Where are there opportunities for you to trailblaze?

2. If you were to break a World Record, how would you feel about the person who later broke your record? How can you ensure that you have a right response when those who come after you achieve even more than you did?

For further thoughts from Matt watch a short video at:

www.livelife123.org/theceilingthefloor

Poem: If Children...

I want to close this section with a very well-known poem that's been floating around for over 50 years. It's a great reminder about the importance of our example to, and influence on, the rising generation.

If children live with criticism,
they learn to condemn.

If children live with hostility,
they learn to fight.

If children live with fear,
they learn to be apprehensive.

If children live with pity,
they learn to feel sorry for themselves.

If children live with ridicule,
they learn to feel shy.

If children live with jealousy,
they learn to feel envy.

If children live with shame,
they learn to feel guilty.

BUT...

If children live with encouragement,
they learn confidence.

If children live with tolerance,
they learn patience.

If children live with praise,
they learn appreciation.

If children live with acceptance,
they learn to love.

If children live with approval,
they learn to like themselves.

If children live with recognition,
they learn it is good to have a goal.

If children live with sharing,
they learn generosity.

If children live with honesty,
they learn truthfulness.

If children live with fairness,
they learn justice.

If children live with kindness and consideration,
they learn respect.

If children live with security,
they learn to have faith in themselves
and in those about them.

If children live with friendliness,
they learn the world is a nice place
in which to live.

Dorothy Law Nolte (1924-2005)

9: Passing on the Baton

I was 11 years old when I decided that I wanted to play the drums. My mum and dad scoured the Yellow Pages to find a great tutor and within a few weeks I was standing at the door of Gerald's house with my mum, waiting for him to answer. In their one phone call, Gerald had asked my mum whether I had any kind of drum to bring with me, to which she enthusiastically responded, "Yes". As the door opened, my new drum teacher smiled and then looked with some disappointment – perhaps even disdain - at the 'drum' I was holding in my hand.

"That's not a drum, that's a tambourine!" he exclaimed.

He was right. It was a tambourine. I look back now and cringe a little. What was my mum thinking?

Anyway, I picked up actual drumming quite well, and my local church very kindly decided to 'try me out' in the worship band. Soon I was playing every Sunday and loving it. Even though I was still very young, I was no longer a spectator at church. I had a role. A responsibility. People trusted me and relied on me.

I remember the time I preached my first sermon in church. Again, the church recognised that I seemed to enjoy talking a lot and, despite concerns about the pleasure I took from the sound of my own voice, they boldly gave me my first Sunday evening preach. My sermon was titled "When the going gets tough" inspired by the Billy Ocean song that had raced to number one in the pop charts earlier that year (this was 1986). Of course it wasn't a very polished performance, and I remember at one point describing how life without God is *"...like a circle that has a bit missing and so isn't really a circle at all."* Truly profound! Even as those words left my lips I remember thinking to myself – that sounds stupid! Despite this, the leaders encouraged me to keep preaching, and I've carried on doing so for the last 26 years.

A year later, the church was launching a brand-new outreach programme to young people. It would be super-high-tech, with computers, video screens, crazy games and relevant and inspiring communication about Jesus. The leaders of this venture – called Prime Time (it sounded really cool in 1987, trust me)

– recognised some leadership ability in me, and so as a 17-year-old I found myself serving as a leader in this exciting new ministry. I was treated as an equal – not an inferior member of the team. My opinions mattered. My ideas counted. In truth, I look back to that time as the moment when the revolution in my faith really happened. Why? Because I was given genuine leadership responsibility, not some token gesture toward it.

A lot has happened in the 25 years since that moment, and as I write this today I feel greatly privileged to now serve the team as the newly-installed Senior Pastor of that Church, Hitchin Christian Centre (www. hcc.org.uk).

What makes that even more special, and amazing, is that the baton of leadership was passed on to me by my own father.

For 31 years Dad led the church as Senior Pastor, serving as a volunteer for the first 20 years and then becoming full-time for the last decade or so. I've learnt more about leadership and baton-passing from my Dad than any other leader on the planet. I've seen our church grow from eight people all those years ago to a community of hundreds today. Why? Because Dad has a baton-carrying commitment in his DNA! He's always been focussed on identifying, developing and releasing other people to take their place in God's world.

Ironically, Dad never wanted me to be a pastor of our church, or of any church for that matter. To be honest, neither did I. Like my sister and my mum, I'd seen the price that my Dad had paid to lead the church; the hurt, disappointment, anger, frustration and brokenness that he has experienced across the years. Why would anyone ever want to be a pastor?

But then, ten years ago, God took me by surprise. I was driving to work and out of nowhere I sensed that God might be speaking to me about leading the church one day. The greatest surprise was the fact that I had an immediate sense of peace about it. It felt right.

So Dad has spent the last ten years investing even more heavily in my leadership. He has given me greater opportunities to speak, lead, and shape the church. All to prepare me for this very moment.

On the evening of Sunday 25th March 2012, this extraordinary baton pass took place. Dad and I stood in front of a heaving church, full of friends and family. It was a very moving service and if you'd permit me to be very personal with you for a moment, I want to share with you what my Dad said to me that evening before he and the leaders of the church commissioned me as Senior Pastor.

Now I assure you that I don't share these words with you in some vain attempt to cheer myself on, but rather to allow you to get a sense of the heart of a baton passer.

When Dad had finished reading these words, he rolled them up and put them inside a metal baton, which he passed to me before he prayed. I carry that baton with me everywhere I go. It's a reminder of not just what I'm called to, but of the leadership example of my Dad – to be willing to step back, at a high personal cost and sacrifice, and pass the baton on to others. Here's what he read:

Matt from Dad – Father to Son

Sunday 25th March 2012

I remember when you were a small boy and your teacher said you held the class in thrall when you gave your weekend news – I knew you would grow up to be a great communicator.

I remember when you knelt on the bottom step in our home and prayed for the salvation of your grandparents and for healing for your dad's cold – I knew you would grow up to be a great prayer warrior.

I remember on New Year's Eve when you said you wanted to make a difference in the coming year — I knew you would reach people for Christ.

I remember when you became the first Head Boy of the Priory School — I knew you would be a leader of men and women.

I remember your loving care for your sister and grandparents — I knew you would have a compassion for people.

I remember how heartbroken you were when a teenage boy you were counselling ran off and you thought there was no hope — I knew you would have a love for young people and a desire to bring them to Christ.

I remember when you gave up a very well paid job to run a Christian Youth Organisation — Crusaders, now Urban Saints — I knew you would impact the lives of many young people nationwide.

I remember when you gave your first sermon — I knew you would speak to the nation.

It is now your time! You have been a P.K. (Pastor's Kid) for long enough. It's time for you to step up! I am so proud of what you have accomplished and I know that you will do great things for God when you carry the baton for HCC.

The best is yet to come –

"To thine own self be true" (Hamlet)

Love Dad
25th March 2012

My hope and prayer is that in everything I do I will continue to honour my dad and never take for granted all he has invested in me. That's worth noting for all those who pick up the baton from others. Honour those who ran before you!

I hope you can see that my own experience, of having a baton passed to me by my Dad, has been life-changing and formative for him and me. Even as I write this I'm profoundly struck by the fact that 2012 is the year that I ended up writing this book. The year the baton of local church leadership passed from Dad to me. The year that an Olympic torch was passed from one person to another all through our country. And the culmination of the opening Olympic ceremony involved some of our greatest athletes passing the torch to a new generation of young athletes who had the privilege of lighting the ultimate torch, declaring the games had begun. God's timing is amazing.

Of course, my Dad stands in a long line of men and women throughout history who have recognised the importance of baton-passing. The Bible is full of examples of people who recognised that the journey of life and faith is about growing yourself; being the best that you can be, and growing others; helping them to be the best that they can be.

Moses passes the baton of leadership to Joshua.

David passes the baton of leadership to Solomon.

Elijah passes the baton of leadership to Elisha.

Mordecai passes the baton of leadership to Esther.

Paul passes the baton of leadership to Timothy.

I've not even mentioned Jesus and the disciples.

This baton pass isn't just between adults. It's to children and young people too.

Throughout both the Old and New Testaments, we see many examples of children and young people being given real responsibility.

Samuel was just a little boy when he started to serve alongside Eli in the Tabernacle.

It's generally accepted that David was between 12 and 16 years old when he took on Goliath.

Josiah became King of Judah at the age of 7.

The servant girl of Naaman's wife was probably just a young teenager when she was courageous enough to speak out and encourage Naaman to go to Elisha for healing.

Jeremiah was just a teen when God called him to be a prophet.

Esther was probably in her late teens when God used her to rescue a whole nation.

Jesus often used children to make powerful points about the nature of the Kingdom.

It's possible that Timothy was in his late teens when he joined Paul in his missionary ministry.

These children and young people were given **real** responsibility.

In fact, when Jeremiah argues with God about being called as a prophet as a child God replies:

> *"Do not say, 'I am only a child.' You must go to everyone I send you to and say whatever I command you. Do not be afraid of them, for I am with you and will rescue you."* (Jeremiah 1:7-8)

It seems that God believes that children and young people have more to offer than just taking round the offering at church now and again. **Whether you are**

young or old, you serve a God who is searching out people to empower, to release; to receive a Kingdom baton that will see them thrive. God has a radar for people of all ages and so should we.

There's a great example of this in Judges 6 where God calls Gideon to become the leader of Israel.

> *"Arise mighty warrior, the Lord is with you," declares the angel of the Lord.*

An interesting exchange then takes place, where Gideon begins to argue on two counts.

Firstly, as far as Gideon is concerned, there's not a huge amount of evidence stacking up that the Lord is with him and the people of God at all. They are being totally oppressed by the Midianite forces; this is not a good time to live in Israel.

Secondly, Gideon scoffs at the idea that he is a 'mighty warrior'. In fact, it seems to me that Gideon is one of the most insecure guys in the Bible. He tells God that his tribe, clan and family are the weakest and most pathetic in the whole of Israel, and if that wasn't enough, Gideon declares himself a 'nobody' (quite literally - it's in the original Hebrew). God calls Gideon a 'mighty warrior'; Gideon believes he's at the very bottom of the pile, the end of the queue, the last guy that anyone would ever pick for their team.

What's going on here?

The answer is simple and it's one of the things that I love about God.

God sees the potential in Gideon. He sees what Gideon will become and He wants to draw it out of him. He challenges Gideon to step up into his destiny. He passes the baton on to Gideon; effectively hollers: "This is your moment to shine Gideon – go for it!"

It's not that God is wearing rose-tinted spectacles when it comes to Gideon. God is fully aware of the faults and failings of this young teen. In fact, if you read the rest of Gideon's story you'll see a man who continues to wrestle with insecurity and doubt.

God is not put off though. God has a 'radar' for potential. He's a baton-carrying God and as His people we have that same responsibility: to see the potential in other people and do all that we can to release it.

In his book *Transforming Children into Spiritual Champions* (Regal, 2003), George Barna reminds us that in most cases "each one of the leaders we respect today was once a child whose potential was identified, shaped and released by those who preceded them as leaders, teachers and other agents of influence."

Someone was seeking out talent. Someone was looking to nurture potential.

Someone was looking to pass the baton on.

We're not *just* talking about leadership here. Ultimately this is about outworking and owning Jesus' command in Matthew 28:18-20 to "make disciples."

We are called to be "followers of Jesus" who *make* "followers of Jesus".

Disciples making disciples. Doing life with people.

I love these words from Paul in 1 Thessalonians 2:8. They capture the very heart of what it means to pour your life in to someone else:

> *"We loved you so much that we were delighted to share with you not only the gospel of God but our lives as well, because you had become so dear to us."*

We 'shared our lives with you!' That's the invitation and the opportunity. You don't have to be working full-time in a charity or church to 'do life' with someone. This is about everyday people connecting with each other in everyday moments. For example, the next time you go shopping why not invite your 'disciple' along and chat together as you're filling up the trolley. You have to eat, right? So maybe once in a while invite your 'disciple' over for dinner with other friends and family; 'do life' together!

We all live such busy lives, so you may be thinking that you don't have time to fit in an investment in someone else. The good news then is that it's not about special times and special places; it's about connecting and investing with people in the everyday moments of our lives. You might think you can't afford to... I'd humbly suggest you can't afford not to!

Today, ask God to give you His 'radar' to identify who you could pass the baton to. **Whether you call yourself a teacher, a mentor, a coach, a discipler – whatever – invest in someone.** Pour your life into somebody. 'Do life' together. Help them become everything God created them to be. Remember, that's what *big* looks like in the Kingdom of God.

PASS THE BATON!

QUESTIONS FOR REFLECTION

1. How good are you at spotting potential? How can you grow in this area?

2. Think again – who could you 'pass the baton' on to?

For further thoughts from Matt watch a short video at:

www.livelife123.org/passthebaton

10: Ten Baton-Passing Tips

So you're committed to 'passing the baton' to others. What are some of the values that need to underpin this? What are you committing yourself to?

You've probably realised by now that this is book doesn't aim to tell you how to practically mentor or disciple someone. There are plenty of great books available on that (some of which I've listed at the back of this one).

The purpose of this book is primarily to appeal to your heart. To stoke up some passion in you to be a future changer. My prayer is simply that you're encouraged and inspired to run your race to the very best of your ability and enable others to do the same.

However, here are ten things that I've learnt during the last 20 years of growing other people that I hope you will find helpful.

1. WALK THE TALK

We've talked a lot about this already. Be an example and don't ask someone to do something you're not prepared to do.

2. BE HOLISTIC

I'm a passionate believer in the 'shalom' of the Gospel (Ephesians 6:15). Shalom is the Hebrew word for 'peace'. Yet this description of 'peace' doesn't just mean the absence of strife. It has a far bigger, fuller, richer meaning than that. It speaks about wholeness and wellbeing across every aspect of life. This reminds us that God is interested in our emotional, relational, intellectual, spiritual and physical well-being. So if God is interested in all these areas of our lives then we should be committed to developing them in ourselves and in others. We're not just concerned about whether someone is reading the Bible; we're also focused on any emotional challenges they're facing. We're not just asking them about their prayer life, but also challenging them about their relationships with family, friends and colleagues. This is whole life, 24/7 disciple-making.

3. BE APPROACHABLE AND ACCEPTING

If we're going to 'do life' with other people then we can't be easily shocked, angered or offended. We need to be approachable so that they feel they can share the stuff that really matters with us. I remember being in a small group where a young guy shared very honestly about his struggle with pornography. It was fantastic that he felt it was safe to do so, and thankfully everyone responded with kindness and grace, mindful that we all have different things that we wrestle with.

Paul tells us in Romans 15:7 that we must *'accept each other just as Christ has accepted you'*. I love the definitions in my Greek dictionary for the Greek word for 'accept' in this passage – it means:

> **to take as one's companion**

> **to take by the hand in order to lead aside**

> **to take or receive into one's home, with the guarantee of kindness**

> **to grant access to one's heart**

That's how Jesus accepts us. In Matthew 11:28 Jesus does not say "Come to me when you've smartened yourself up and you've cleaned up the mess and brokenness of your life." He simply says *"Come to me...Come to me, all who are weary and burdened and I will give you rest."*

You see, Jesus understands the difference between acceptance and agreement. You may disagree with the way that someone is living their life, or the decisions that they are making, but you can still accept them; you can still love them. Love and acceptance build trust, and this is what earns you the right to challenge someone.

4. BE CHALLENGING

Being approachable doesn't mean that you don't offer challenge. I want to be someone who, in genuine love and compassion, has the courage to say the tough things to the people who I'm helping to grow. Stuff like: "Get over yourself and grow up! Sort yourself out. Don't do that - that's going to hurt you. Bad idea!"

Paul gives an example of this in Galatians 2:11-14 when he describes challenging the disciple Peter's behaviour:

> *"But when Peter came to Antioch, I had to oppose him to his face, for what he did was very wrong. When he first arrived, he ate with the Gentile Christians,*

> *who were not circumcised. But afterward, when*
> *some friends of James came, Peter wouldn't eat with*
> *the Gentiles anymore. He was afraid of criticism*
> *from these people who insisted on the necessity*
> *of circumcision. As a result, other Jewish Christians*
> *followed Peter's hypocrisy, and even Barnabas was*
> *led astray by their hypocrisy. When I saw that they*
> *were not following the truth of the gospel message,*
> *I said to Peter in front of all the others..."*

So Paul goes on to challenge Peter about his behaviour. Why? Not because they're rivals. Because he wants Peter to grow, to be the best that he can be.

I am always struck by how John tells us in John 1:14 that Jesus is *"full of grace and truth."* We see how this plays out in the story of the woman caught in the act of adultery (John 8:1-11). Jesus tells her He doesn't condemn her (grace) but goes on to challenge her to change her way of life (truth). We need to be grace and truth people. Approachable, but still challenging people to grow and change, empowered by the Holy Spirit and encouraged by us.

Author and speaker Tony Campolo once said "If we lose this generation of young people, as we surely are losing them, we will lose them, not because we have made Christianity too hard them but because we have made Christianity too easy for them – and the reality is that this easy Christianity is not the biblical Christianity - for the Jesus of scripture expects much more of us."

5. BE CAREFUL OF YOUR OWN NEEDS

It's very easy to get to a place where someone can become dependent on you. This is not just bad for them; it's also not good for you. We have to be so careful that we don't enter in to baton-passing relationships to feed our self-esteem or self-worth. Our identity is in Christ, not in the thoughts or feelings of others.

6. BE A LISTENER

To some people – like me - this can be a real challenge. I quickly find myself ready to respond to what someone is saying before they've finished saying it, rather than giving them 100% of my attention. To be an active listener is to fully engage with what someone is saying without considering your response. The late Steven Covey, in his best selling book, *The Seven Habits of Highly Effective People*, speaks about the importance of "seeking first to understand, before being understood." That's good advice.

I love the way that Henri Nouwen writes about the profound nature of true listening:

> *"To care means first of all to be present to each other. From experience you know that those who care for you become present to you. When they listen, they listen to you. When they speak, they speak to you. Their presence is a healing presence because they accept you on your terms, and they encourage you to take your own life seriously."*

- Henri Nouwen, from Out of Solitude (1984)

7. DON'T OFFER EASY ANSWERS AND SPIRITUAL CLICHÉS

The truth is that there are no easy answers to some of the struggles we face in life. I remember the first ever funeral I conducted, a few years ago. John was a great guy in his early fifties who had died from a recurrence of liver cancer. He left a wonderful wife and two fantastic teenage boys. I've given a number of sermons over the years on suffering, yet in moments like this words fail you. Easy answers and spiritual clichés do more damage than good. Job's friends did a great job at the start by offering comfort and support. They sat in the silence with him. It was only when they opened their mouths that they got themselves in trouble.

8. DON'T MOVE PEOPLE ON TOO SLOWLY... OR TOO QUICKLY

Real wisdom and discernment are needed to understand when and how to stretch people. You don't want to give someone so much responsibility that you set them up to fail; at the same time you don't want to give them so little responsibility that they don't grow. A helpful way of approaching this sometimes is to ask people to grade themselves in a certain area between 1 and 10. If they rate themselves a 6 – for example – then explore with them what it would mean for them to move to a 7. Step-by-step change keeps them moving and growing, but at the right pace for them.

9. YOU'RE NOT MAKING A CLONE OF YOURSELF

You are not creating 'mini me'. You're helping someone fulfil *their* God-given potential; you're helping *them* to become like Jesus. We all know the famous story in which David takes on Goliath in 1 Samuel 17. Before the big fight begins, King Saul tries to give David his royal armour – but it doesn't fit; it just weighs David down. David needs to do things his own way and not become Saul.

We need to be careful that we're not imposing

stuff on to the next generation that doesn't fit them. Sometime this can be the baggage of our own opinions and limitations. We need to have the courage to let this stuff go, so that they can be released to do things their way.

10. GIVE PEOPLE THE FREEDOM TO TAKE RISKS AND SOMETIMES FAIL

I love the fact that Jesus constantly takes risks with His disciples. He sends them out and gives them regular opportunities to step outside their comfort zones. The story of Peter walking on water in Matthew 14 is a great reminder of what happens when we respond to Jesus' risk-embracing invitation. Peter enjoys the incredible elation of a water-walking moment which a few seconds later is matched by the deep disappointment of nearly drowning. Jesus is there in both the success and the failure, and of course we, like Peter, learn from both.

We generally learn more quickly from our failures. We naturally ask ourselves: What did I do wrong? How do I make sure this doesn't happen again? How do I make sure I move on and don't live in this failure moment?

Learning from success can be far more difficult.

Success quickly breeds pride and overconfidence. I remember speaking to one of my Spiritual Directors a few years back and telling him about how I'd recently met a national Christian leader who was known for his prophetic gifting. I informed my Spiritual Director - with no small amount of pride I have to confess - that this prophet had told me that I was 'amazing'. I'll never forget my Spiritual Director's response: "Matt...you're not amazing."

Some of you might think he was being harsh. The truth was that he was rightly seeking to crush the ugly emergence of pride in my life. Bearing in mind that the scriptures tell us that God opposes the proud (James 4:6), I'm pretty glad he was all over this like a rash.

I hope these ten pointers give you some initial help as you think about investing in someone. There are some great resources and books out there which will take things much further but I saw no point in duplicating them. I've put loads of examples of these on the www.livelife123.org web site, which I'll introduce you to in a moment.

So, you've run your race, and run it well.

You've passed on the baton, growing the person as best you can.

Now what do you do? Do you go back to the changing room and consider your job done?

Not on your life! Have you ever seen a relay team do that? Nope.

The final thing you need to do if you're going to be someone who changes the future, is to cheer the next runners like crazy.

QUESTIONS FOR REFLECTION

1. Which of these ten tips did you find most helpful/ challenging? Why?

2. What practically might you change in your approach after reading this list?

3. How much of a struggle is pride for you? What will you do to keep it under control?

4. Who is mentoring you? Who do you go to for honest advice and direction about the big stuff?

For further thoughts from Matt watch a short video at:

www.livelife123.org/toptentips

11: Cheer Like Crazy

I remember when the African Children's choir came to our church. Our building had never been so rammed full of people. It was hot and sweaty, and the five large ceiling fans could not avert the tangy smell of over three hundred of us, packed together like past-their-sell-by-date sardines. It didn't matter. We were all too inspired and moved by the courage and passion of this mini choir to worry about the heat and the smell.

There was one unforgettable moment that stands out from that evening. At one point in the concert, as the music continued to blare, the children took turns to walk up to the microphone and introduce themselves. Before rejoining the group, each one proudly declared what they dreamed of doing when they grew up.

"My name is Nishimwee, and one day I'm going to be a lawyer."

The crowd cheered.

"My name is Koyejo, and one day I'm going to be doctor."

More cheers.

"My name is Maisha, and one day I'm going to be Prime Minister."

Further cheers, and the odd "oooh!"

As the crowd whooped with encouragement, something inside me wanted to jump up and shout back to these bundles of potential:

"YES! Go for it! Dream big. Believe big. Your God is a God with big dreams. You were born for reason. With God nothing is impossible."

I want to be a cheerleader to, and for, the rising generation.

Why? Because young people are way too often demonised in the media. The church needs to be more vocal nationally and locally in cheering them on, in order to ensure that the press and media doesn't create a self-fulfilling prophecy.

The really sad fact is that sometimes, the church is the *last* place that people of all ages experience encouragement; yet the church should be leading the way.

I get weary with the self-righteous Pharisees who seem to have been 'blessed' with the gift of complaining and the ministry of pointing out mistakes.

I remember speaking at a church one evening, when as the service came to a close I publicly thanked the hosting team, who had done an amazing job of looking after everybody. This seemed like the right thing to do. To say thank you and show appreciation; to encourage the people who had worked hard to make the event such a great success.

Sadly however, not everybody agreed.

As the crowd dispersed after the final song I spotted a very angry looking man walking down the centre aisle towards me. I was hoping that he was suffering from a severe form of facial sunburn (not that I would wish that on anybody, you understand) but as I was about to discover, his face was actually red with rage.

"How could you do that?" he exclaimed.

"Do what?" I asked, my brain whirring to think of what I could possibly have said or done to have caused such offence.

"Rob those people of their heavenly reward", he

replied. "You thanked those people for hosting us and because of that you robbed them of their reward before God!"

Since they say that confession is good for the soul, can I make a confession? I wanted to 'lay hands on him.' You'll be pleased to know that I am not a violent man, so I restrained myself, but there still followed a long debate about whether it was right to thank and encourage people for the job that they were doing.

I didn't win over my tomato-faced friend that evening. He eventually turned and left, and for a while I stood there wondering what on earth had just happened.

Hopefully you will agree that his was a pretty severe and unnecessary – even unbiblical – reaction to my desire to encourage and cheer on the hosts. Still, I get anxious at times that we simply aren't good enough at the ministry of encouragement in the church today. "Must try harder," as my Chemistry teacher used to say.

Everybody needs encouragement. We all need cheerleaders. We all need to know that there are people who have our backs. Who are the people who won't let a bad word be said about us? Who are the people who are the first to applaud and the last to complain?

Consider for a few moments your response to the following questions:

> **Are you someone who helps people to grow? Or are you someone who causes people to shrink?**

> **Are the relationships you have with people dictated by your need to get something from them, or are your relationships with people primarily about your passion to see them flourish and succeed?**

> **Are you a good person to be with? Do you build people up? When people have spent time with you, do they feel bigger, better, bolder and more beautiful? Or do they feel smaller, discouraged, fearful, disappointed and even useless?**

I want to live a life that *cheers people on*. I want to be someone who inspires and motivates people to grow. I want to encourage people not to settle for mediocrity or the status quo, but to embrace God's healing power and radical adventure for their life.

There's a great example of this in 1 Samuel 14. The Israelite people are being threatened by the Philistine nation. So Jonathan – the son of Israel's King, Saul - boldly decides to check out the enemy. So we're told in verses 6-7:

> *"Jonathan said to his young armour-bearer, 'Come, let's go over to the outpost of those uncircumcised fellows. Perhaps the LORD will act on our behalf. Nothing can hinder the LORD from saving, whether by many or by few.' 'Do all that you have in mind,' his armour-bearer said. 'Go ahead; I am with you heart and soul.'"*

I want to be like that armour-bearer. Someone who inspires people to do great things; to be the best that they can be.

We see the importance of this time and time again throughout Scripture.

In Joshua chapter one, it wasn't enough for Joshua to hear God telling him three times to "Be strong and courageous' (Joshua 1:6,7,9). He needed that encouragement from the people too (1:18).

In Hebrews 12, the chapter that follows the incredible roll-call of men and women of faith, the writer reminds us that we're being cheered on by a multitude who have journeyed before us:

> *"Do you see what this means - all these pioneers who blazed the way, all these veterans cheering us on? It means we'd better get on with it. Strip down, start running - and never quit! No extra spiritual*

fat, no parasitic sins. Keep your eyes on Jesus, who both began and finished this race we're in. Study how he did it. Because he never lost sight of where he was headed - that exhilarating finish in and with God - he could put up with anything along the way: Cross, shame, whatever. And now he's there, in the place of honour, right alongside God. When you find yourselves flagging in your faith, go over that story again, item by item, that long litany of hostility he plowed through. That will shoot adrenaline into your souls!" - Hebrews 12:1-3 (The Message)

Paul was an amazing cheer-leader for Timothy, and his last two letters, written from death row, give loads of examples of his commitment to inspire and cheer Timothy on to great things. Time and time again Paul is saying to Timothy "You can do it!"

The challenge today is to consider every interaction that you have with people and honestly ask yourself the question: am I helping these people to become bigger or smaller? Am I helping people or hurting people? Am I building people up... or blowing them up?

A few years back, Tom Rath and Donald O Clifton wrote a book called *How Full is Your Bucket? – Positive Strategies for Work and Life*. Rath and Clifton suggested that everyone has an invisible 'bucket.' This bucket represents the level of healthy emotions and thoughts connected to a positive self worth. It'll come as no surprise that Rath and Clifton summise that we are at our best when our buckets are overflowing... and our worst when they are empty.

The key question that the book asks is this: are you someone who fills other people's buckets, or you someone who takes from other people's buckets?

This question is really important, because the answer could have a massive affect on the lives of those we interact with.

Many years ago, a professor called Dr Elizabeth Hurlock conducted an experiment to see what impact different kinds of feedback would have on the maths performance of 10 and 11-year-olds. She wanted to find out if it was more effective to praise, criticise or ignore pupils. Every day, the pupils were given a test – and every day they were given feedback on their results. The children were split into three groups; one group was praised; one group was criticised and one group was ignored. By the end of the week, the group who were being praised had improved their maths performance by 71%. The group who were constantly criticised had only improved their performance by 19%, and the group who were completely ignored had only improved their performance by 5%

This stuff is really important – it has a massive effect on people's lives.

It's so easy for us to take each other for granted. When was the last time that you went out of your way to say thank you to someone; to show your appreciation for something they did? When did you last cheer someone on?

The Apostle Paul was always expressing thanks for people:

> *"I thank my God through Jesus Christ for all of you, because your faith is being reported all over the world"* (Romans 1:8)

> *"I always thank God for you"* (1 Corinthians 1:4)

> *"...ever since I heard about your faith in the Lord Jesus and your love for all the saints, I have not stopped giving thanks for you."* (Ephesians 1:15-16)

> *"I thank my God every time I remember you."* (Philippians 1:6)

> *"We always thank God, the Father of our Lord Jesus Christ, when we pray for you, because we have heard*

of your faith in Christ Jesus..." (Colossians 1:3-4)

"How can we thank God enough for you in return for all the joy we have in the presence of our God because of you?" (1 Thessalonians 3:9)

"I thank God, whom I serve... as night and day I constantly remember you in my prayers. Recalling your tears, I long to see you, so that I may be filled with joy" (2 Timothy 1:3-4)

"I always thank my God as I remember you in my prayers, because I hear about your faith in the Lord Jesus and your love for all the saints" (Philemon 1:4-5)

Paul understood that if you want to see people thrive, you have to appreciate them. When we appreciate something it, literally speaking, goes up in value. Everyone wants to be appreciated. Appreciation gives us the fuel to help us keep on going, particularly during the tough times.

A few years ago Urban Saints ran a leaders' chill-out zone at a large youth event at Alton Towers. As leaders came into the chill-out zone we gave each of them a small box of chocolates. One lady was very taken aback and asked why we were giving her chocolates. We told her that it was because we recognised that being a youth leader was really tough; we knew it was hard work and that sometimes she probably felt like she was getting nowhere. The chocolates were a small way of us saying thank you; thank you for everything you're doing to grow young people. As we said these words, she burst into tears. Then she told us: "In all the years that I have led my youth group, no-one has ever said thank you".

Don't you want to be a person who appreciates people? To be someone who is always looking for things that others do well – big or small – and to cheer them on and say "well done"?

The old mantra is true: behaviour that's rewarded gets repeated.

So commit yourself to being a cheer-leader today.

Cheer others on until your throat is hoarse; until your arms are tired; until your smile might cause your face to crack. Because if you do, you'll give the generation who follow you the courage to keep on, keeping on, whatever life may throw at them – because they know they have you in their corner!

QUESTIONS FOR REFLECTION

1. How good are you at supporting and encouraging others? How could you improve in this area?

2. Who should you already be cheering on? Who do you find difficult to cheer because of pride or jealousy? How will you address this?

For further thoughts from Matt watch a short video at:

www.livelife123.org/cheerlikecrazy

12: Never Give Up

Picture the scene:

An old man is lying on his death bed.
His breathing is becoming harder and shallower.
It seems like he's trying to say something, so one
who is close to him leans forward and places
their ear to his frail mouth.
"Bring me a child," the old man whispers.
Why?
Because even in his dying, final breaths, the
man wants to speak words of life, hope and
encouragement over the generation to come.

That's the picture I always see in my mind's eye
when I read the words of Psalm 71:18. This is the
heartbeat of that old man:

> *"Even when I am old and grey, do not forsake me,
> O God, till I declare your power to the next
> generation, your might to all who are to come."*

God, in my dying breath, may I be someone who cheers on the next generation.

This book has sought to inspire you to be someone who doesn't make history, but changes the future.

To be someone who recognises that the God we serve is in the business of changing eternal destinies, transforming the whole of creation and ushering in a bright future.

To be someone who recognises that in the Kingdom of God, *big* is when you commit yourself wholeheartedly to change even one person's life.

To be someone who breaks the curse of comparison and is committed to run **their** race, and not waste time looking over their shoulder at others.

To be someone who is committed to run their race **well**, stretching themselves so that their example will stretch others.

To be someone who is committed to pass on the baton, with a radar for potential in other people; helping them to become all that God created them to be, and 'doing life' together.

To be someone who is committed to being a cheer-leader, building others up through every interaction.

To be someone who keeps on, keeping on; who never quits, even when life gets tough. Why? Because you know that your life is in God's hands. You understand that He is the author and the finisher of your faith. That what He started in you, He will finish. That His power - made perfect in your weakness - means that nothing is impossible.

So in all that we do, we remember:

> *"...with all this going for us, my dear, dear friends, stand your ground. And don't hold back. Throw yourselves into the work of the Master, confident that nothing you do for him is a waste of time or effort"* 1 Corinthians 15:58 (The Message)

QUESTIONS FOR REFLECTION

1. Are you prepared to pick up this vision, and run with it for yourself?

2. What does it mean to 'throw yourself into the work of the Master' now?

 For further thoughts from Matt watch a short video at:

www.livelife123.org/nevergiveup

13: The Call to Live Life 1-2-3

So how do you put all this baton-carrying stuff into practice?

How do you change the future?

I've been living with a little idea for a while now that I've been sharing with a few close friends. Now I want to share it with you.

It's a call to live life 1-2-3 and it looks like this.

Imagine you invite ONE person to be your guide. Someone you're learning from. Someone who can help and challenge you to become everything that God created you to be. For me, this is a guy called Peter Gilbert. I've been meeting with Pete three times a year for 24 hours at a time, for the last five years. Pete reads all my journals and he knows almost everything about me. I'm very thankful that I can trust him not to tweet my failings to the world. I'm committed to learning from Pete about what it means to be a better husband, father, friend, leader, and most importantly, follower of Jesus Christ. Pete and I had known each other for a few years before we got to a place where I recognised Pete could help me in all these areas. Can you find at least ONE person that you can **learn** from in that kind of a way?

Then, what if you were to ask TWO people to be your 'running mates'? People who you share your life with; being open about your real struggles; your inner and secret life. These are mutually-accountable, challenging, real relationships. My two are Phil and John. They know me well, see me regularly, know they have permission to challenge me and choose to encourage me. They help me put in to practice what Pete is teaching me. Can you find at least TWO people that you can **do life** with?

Finally, what if you were willing to pass on the baton of faith to THREE other people - equipping them to become all that God created them to be, living like Jesus in the world? You'd be inspiring each of them to share their faith with others; disciples making disciples. As I write, I'm trying to do this with three teenage guys in my church (Joshua, Will and Tayo). We seek to catch up every couple of weeks and chat about all aspects of faith and life. Can you find at least THREE people that you can **pass the baton** to?

I want to suggest that **everybody** could 'Live Life 1-2-3'. It's a practical outworking of everything I've written in this book. The ages of any of the people in the relationships I've described aren't prescribed or important. You may be 50 years old and your 'THREE' are all in their 30s or 20s. Or maybe they're older than you. The point is, you're making a commitment to **Learn** (from your 1), **do Life** (with your 2), and **Lead** (your 3).

I would go so far as to say that I believe – passionately - that we will never fulfil our potential in God without these kinds of relationships in place.

As I've said earlier in this book, I have a particular passion for reaching young people. To this end, if we were to specifically embrace this way of life to address the challenge of reaching the rising generation of children and young people, it could bring about seismic change within 20 years. Let me tell you why:

Do you know that there are nine million children and young people, within the UK and Ireland, who pretty much only know 'Jesus' as a swear word. If they stood in a line, it would stretch from Lands End to John O'Groats not once – not twice - but three times. This generation are drowning in a tsunami of consumerism. They're written off by the media. They're wrestling with destructive lifestyle choices, impacted by family breakdown and, while many churches are working hard to reach out, HALF of our churches have no provision for children and young people at all.

What if this could be turned around? Could we change the future? Not just for this generation, but for those not even born?

If just a hundred youth leaders committed to 'Live Life 1-2-3', then in year one we'd be investing in 300 young people. If those 300 caught the vision and did likewise, there would be over 1,200 people in these intentional disciple-making relationships in the second year. By the end of year three, there could be 3,900; by the end of year four, 12,000, and so on. Within only a decade, the church could see over two million children and young people become followers of Jesus.

Two million children and young people who were passionate followers of Jesus would change a whole generation. In fact, it could breach the tipping point to change a whole nation. Who knows what the global consequences might be?

It may take longer. Maybe twenty years is more

realistic, Yet I believe it is perfectly possible that we could see two million children and young people deciding to Live Life 1-2-3. Why would we aim for anything less?

I want to challenge and inspire you to embrace this commitment for yourself. To surround yourself with intentional, accountable, reproducing, disciple-making relationships.

If you're up for it, then don't waste any time. Get stuck in and share the challenge with others.

Right here, I want to invite you to write in the names of some potential 1s, 2s and 3s. This isn't binding (you can write it in pencil if you like), but hopefully it will get you started. Take a few moments to pray, asking God to help you as you consider which people He might be drawing you into deeper, more intentional discipleship relationships with.

My ONE – from whom I will commit to **Learn,** and to whom I will commit to listen – could be:

My TWO – who I commit to 'do Life' with; sharing myself in total honesty – could be:

My THREE – who I will seek to positively **Lead** into a deeper walk with God, and into their own disciple-making – could be:

To sign up to become part of the 'Live Life 1-2-3' movement and discover resources, tools and inspiration to help you on your baton-passing journey, go to www.livelife123.org today. Plus - FOLLOW on Twitter @livelife123org and LIKE the Facebook page www.facebook.com/livelife123org.

For those of you who are now looking for more 'how to' information then www.livelife123.org is a great next stop.

 For further thoughts from Matt watch a short video at:

www.livelife123.org/livelife123

14: Re-imagining the Future

I hope that this short book has encouraged and challenged you to be someone who changes the future, one life at a time. If we all commit to this, then maybe this dream; this vision statement which I wrote back in November 2000, might come true in my lifetime:

I'm dreaming of a rising generation who are released to take their place and have their voice, stepping up and taking responsibility for their life and their world.

I'm dreaming of a rising generation who understand that Jesus calls them into a radical, risk-embracing, world-changing, danger-accepting adventure: 24/7, whole-life discipleship.

I'm dreaming of a rising generation whose creativity is fanned into flame, pioneering what we can't even imagine, birthing new expressions of church to reach those we cannot reach.

I'm dreaming of a rising generation who have the freedom to take risks – knowing that sometimes they'll succeed and other times they'll fail – but learning so much from both.

I'm dreaming of a rising generation who challenge this dominant consumer culture, becoming Kingdom invaders, living lives of justice and generosity.

I'm dreaming of a rising generation who do more with God, and more for God, than we could ever imagine – understanding that the qualifications for becoming a transformational leader are brokenness, weakness, vulnerability and availability.

I'm dreaming of a rising generation who are healed and whole – that it is well with their soul.

I'm dreaming of a rising generation who become all that God created them to be; that they would fly, that they would soar; that our ceiling would become their floor.

I'm dreaming of a rising generation who learn, love and live the Word of God.

I'm dreaming of a rising generation who live supernatural, extraordinary, miraculous lives in the power of God's Spirit.

I'm dreaming of a rising generation whose lives

shine like stars, showing everyone they meet the best way of living life, with grace and truth; making Jesus famous wherever they go.

I'm dreaming of a rising generation who become passionate, unswerving baton carriers of the Kingdom to every generation, with their eye of influence on the unborn child.

This is the new reality that I long for! And I'm committing the rest of my life to that cause. It was George Bernard-Shaw who famously said:

> *"Some men see things as they are and ask, 'why?'*
> *I dream of things that never were and ask, 'why not?'"*

So can a nation be changed? Can a generation rise up and change their country and culture?

As the watchmen and women that God has set over this generation of children and young people, dare we declare... **why not?**

For further thoughts from Matt watch a short video at:

www.livelife123.org/reimagine

15: Read, Watch, Respond

As you embrace a commitment to change the future – and perhaps to Live Life 1-2-3 – can I boldly close by asking you to consider making your first sacrifice right now? Would you make a donation, big or small, which will go to two invaluable causes which aim to change the future (particularly if you received this book for FREE)?

The first 50% of your donation will go toward producing ongoing resources, support and training for the LiveLife123.org website. You'll get the benefit of this so a one-off donation will really help. We can't run the website on air.

The second 50% of your donation will support the work of a brilliant emerging leaders organisation in Africa which has a vision to train four million new leaders in up to 30 African nations by 2020; inspiring them to find sustainable solutions to the poverty and unemployment in their communities.

This organisation is called Emerging Leaders and you'll find more information on them in the coming pages.

If we're serious about seeing the future change in our nation then we must be willing to invest not just our time, but also our money, in the generations to come.

So before you embark on this adventure to be a future changer please start by making a sacrifice. Whether you give £3, £10 or £20 doesn't matter. It's your heart that counts! You can donate in two ways:

Online – www.livelife123.org/give

Text 'AONE23 £3' to 70070
(Other possible amounts are £1, £2, £4, £5 and £10)

I hope this request does not offend you. You don't have to give. I just hope you can spare at least £3.

Please respond today, right now if you can.

Thank you so much.

So again, here are the details...

www.livelife123.org/give

Text 'AONE23 £3' to 70070

Urban Saints

Since 1906 Urban Saints (formerly known as Crusaders) has been reaching out to children and young people with the good news of Jesus Christ. We are passionate about working with all children and young people, helping them realise their full God-given potential as they journey from childhood to adulthood.

OUR PASSION...

...to help young people live lives of faith, hope and love through Jesus Christ.

OUR DREAM...

...to release a movement of radical young people who will take the good news to every generation.

OUR CULTURE...

Riotous FUN

Being a Christian is not dull and boring! We believe that followers of Jesus should show the world how to really party.

Adventurous FAITH

Jesus doesn't invite His followers to 'play it safe'.

He calls us into a radical, risk-embracing, world-changing, danger accepting, servant-hearted adventure.

So we wholeheartedly throw ourselves into the Father's embrace, the Son's mission and the Spirit's power.

Genuine FRIENDSHIP
Who wants to do stuff alone? Not us! We're following Jesus with friends because we recognise we need each other.

Life in all its FULLNESS
God wants us to be fully alive. So we embrace a life of learning and growing in order to realise our God-given potential through a healthy rhythm of rest, play and work.

OUR WORK
Equipping the Church

Urban Saints supports over 1,000 churches across the UK and Ireland with our leading edge training and resources website Energize. A complete toolkit to reach and disciple a generation, Energize is literally bursting with a huge range of resources, including:

> A continual stream of adaptable, creative, biblically-based meeting plans for 3-4s, 5-6s, 7-10s, 11-14s and 15+.

> A powerful search tool to look for activities, games, crafts etc. from the huge Energize database of ideas.

> 'Easy to use' drama sketches to complement meeting plans.

> On-line training courses for leaders, whatever their level of experience – all materials provided including PowerPoint slides.

> On-line training courses for teenagers to encourage them to begin helping in a youth/children's group.

> An extensive range of articles to inspire, encourage and resource leaders for the demanding role of working with children and young people.

> Articles to keep leaders up-to-date with best practice guidelines and legislation affecting volunteers working with children and young people.

See **www.urbansaints.org/energizeintro** for more information.

Offering life-changing experiences

Children and young people can attend a variety of experiences including special events, holidays, and overseas community projects and training programmes. These are often life-changing, defining moments, where young people can really get to grips with what it means to know and love God.

See **www.urbansaints.org/experiences** for more information.

Become an Urban Saints Partner

We can't all be youth workers, but we can still play our part to help children and young people fulfil their God-given potential.

By becoming an Urban Saints Partner you will enable us to...

> Establish and support youth and children's groups across the UK and Ireland

> Provide effective training for volunteer youth and children's leaders

> Develop adaptable, creative resources to share faith with children and young people

> Run life-changing experiences for children and young people

> Develop the leaders of tomorrow by training

young people as leaders today

> Act as a catalyst to help churches work together
to achieve more in their community

See **www.urbansaints.org/partners** for more
information.

**For more information on the work of Urban Saints
contact us at:**

Urban Saints Support Centre:
Kestin House, 45 Crescent Road,
Luton, Beds. LU2 0AH

01582 589850

01582 721702

email@urbansaints.org

www.urbansaints.org

www.twitter.com/urbansaints

www.facebook.com/urbansaints

www.livelife123.org

Emerging Leaders

The vision of Emerging Leaders is to bring the best leadership development to the grassroots of Africa. We believe that strong leadership acts as a catalyst to youth employment and prosperity. Leadership exists to benefit others. By taking the best leadership principles to the grassroots, we help people find sustainable solutions to poverty and unemployment in their own communities.

Our three-phased strategy aims to delivers a self-sustaining, scalable programme of leadership development for all youth of sub-Saharan Africa.

PHASE 1: Gaining entry
PHASE 2: Pilot - run to ensure the concept works
PHASE 3: Go nationwide

A robust and efficient strategy is vital for Emerging Leaders to expand across nations. The support and commitment from our local partners is crucial in every step of the project, and makes it possible to enter and expand in three new countries every year.

Building on our continued success, by 2020 Emerging Leaders wants to be touching hearts and minds of all youth in 30 African nations and have taken the first steps to expansion in the West.

Emerging Leaders is committed to the highest quality programs that provide the greatest benefits to youth in the developing world. We make substantial investments in monitoring and evaluation of the success of our programmes to ensure the anticipated benefits are achieved.

> Track project information to ensure that we work effectively toward our goals and objectives

> Identify strengths and weaknesses to inform program decisions and make timely improvements

> Provide accurate and timely information about progress toward desired objectives to our stakeholders

> Investigate opportunities to understand our program environment and improve our ongoing program implementation and future program planning

Our in-country staff and partners visit our programs regularly to gather information about program effectiveness, provide support to students and communities, and highlight areas for future improvement. We use a variety of methods, such as interviews and surveys with key stakeholders, such as students and community leaders, to support us in our monitoring activities.

For more information see **www.emerging-leaders.net**

What people are saying about Emerging Leaders:

Tobias Nyondo, Global Grants Compliance Director, World Vision

"Many leadership courses are very expensive and thereby limit potential leaders to realize and sharpen their skills. Emerging Leaders has brought the rare training of leaders closer to the people that need it. Malawi is engulfed with abject poverty, low self-esteem individuals and envy on one hand and warm, receptive, open minded individuals and a new generation with a deep desire to do things different on the other hand. It is this target group that Emerging Leaders is reaching out to and the nation is destined to a new and greater level of improved leadership. The more potential leaders

are exposed to such practical and clear leadership trainings the more improved their skills will be and the healthier the nation."

Victor Mughogho, Executive Director, Eagles Relief and Development Programme

"It was the best leadership coaching session I have ever attended. I believe the greatest need for Africa right now and in the future is leadership development. Africa has been a recipient of many donations but still remains stagnant in many fields. The greatest and best donation that Africa needs is leadership development. This is why Emerging Leaders is so relevant. It is visionary leadership that will take Africa out of poverty. Leadership development is the secret to Africa's future, the key to releasing Africa's massive potential. The poverty of Africa is not one of resources, but it is a poverty of leadership. As President Johnson-Sirleaf of Liberia, said: "Africa is not poor. It is poorly managed."

Johnnie McMillan, VegPro, Kenya

"In my 12 years of working in Africa, by far the most rewarding experience has been the three days spent assisting Emerging Leaders deliver a training

programme to 100 of our workers. To witness fundamental shifts in understanding that create a sense of hope in those that have lost hope is not only moving, but powerful. Powerful in the sense of what can be achieved within our communities and also within our business where mobilising & truly empowering a workforce may prove to be game changing."

Patrick Mwale, Executive Director, COYIDA, Malawi

"Emerging Leaders uses a very innovative and strategic management trainer approach. They teach with great enthusiasm and their curriculum is fit for all levels, be it at a very grassroot organisations as well as big and advanced management and leadership. Our local partners in Mzimba will never forget the wonderful leadership tactics that were taught."

Vincent Moyo, Country Representative for Malawi Tearfund, Malawi

"Leadership development is central to seeing Malawi overcome poverty especially now when as a young democracy Malawi is having to fight corruption and dictatorship tendencies in most sections of the

society. Your work creates hope for a new generation of leaders who are there to sacrifice and serve their people with passion and reverence, is ordained by God and starts with oneself. It deals with issues of greed and selfishness while challenging leaders to unite and look at the bigger picture that would bring lasting positive change. I am committed to support the initiative in the best possible way I can."

Recommended further reading

Geeks and Geezers: How Era, Values and Defining Moments Shape Leaders
Warren Bennis and Robert J Thomas
(Harvard Business School Press, 2002)

Growing Young Leaders: A Practical Guide to Mentoring Teens
Ruth Hassall (BRF, 2009)

Baton Change: Releasing the Next Generation
Peter Lyne (Sovreign World, 2000)

Mentoring to develop disciples and leaders
John Mallison (Scripture Union Australia, 1998)

Developing the leaders around you
John C Maxwell (Trust Media Distribution, 1995)

How full is your bucket?
Tom Rath and Donald O Clifton (Gallup Press, 2005)

Spiritual Leadership: A Commitment to Excellence for Every Believer
J Oswald Sanders (Moody Press, 1970)

Connecting: The Mentoring Relationships you Need to Succeed in Life
Paul D. Stanley and J Robert Clinton (NavPress, 1992)

To Plant a Walnut Tree: How to Create a Fruitful Legacy by Using your Experience
Trevor Waldock (Nicholas Brealey Publishing, 2011)